Chaucer

Chaucer

David Aers

Lecturer in English Literature
University of East Anglia

16962

HUMANITIES PRESS INTERNATIONAL, INC.
Atlantic Highlands, NJ

First published in 1986 in the United States of America by
HUMANITIES PRESS INTERNATIONAL, INC.,
Atlantic Highlands, NJ 07716

© David Aers, 1986

Library of Congress Cataloging-in-Publication Data

Aers, David.
  Chaucer.

  (Harvester new readings)
  Bibliography: p.
  1. Chaucer, Geoffrey, d. 1400—Criticism and
interpretation. I. Title. II. Series.
PR1924.A47 1986   821'.1   86-268
ISBN 0-391-03420-0

PRINTED IN GREAT BRITAIN

To the Memory of Elizabeth Salter
Teacher, Scholar and Friend

Harvester New Readings

This major new series offers a range of important new critical introductions to English writers, responsive to new bearings which have recently emerged in literary analysis. Its aim is to make more widely current and available the perspectives of contemporary literary theory, by applying these to a selection of the most widely read and studied English authors.

The range of issues covered varies with each author under survey. The series as a whole resists the adoption of general theoretical principles, in favour of the candid and original application of the critical and theoretical models found most appropriate to the survey of each individual author. The series resists the representation of any single either traditionally or radically dominant discourse, working rather with the complex of issues which emerge from a close and widely informed reading of the author in question in his or her social, political and historical context.

The perspectives offered by these lucid and accessible introductory books should be invaluable to students seeking an understanding of the full range and complexity of the concerns of key canonical writers. The major concerns of each author are critically examined and sympathetically and lucidly reassessed, providing indispensable handbooks to the work of major English authors seen from new perspectives.

David Aers	*Chaucer*
Drummond Bone	*Byron*
Angus Calder	*T.S. Eliot*
Simon Dentith	*George Eliot*
Kelvin Everest	*Keats*
Kate Flint	*Dickens*
Paul Hamilton	*Wordsworth*
Brean Hammond	*Pope*
Kiernan Ryan	*Shakespeare*
Simon Shepherd	*Spenser*
Nigel Wood	*Swift*

Contents

Acknowledgements

I should like to thank the many people who have enabled the writing of this book, including other writers and influences who could never be adequately reflected in the notes and brief bibliography. I should like especially to thank Kelvin Everest for his support and Yvonne McGregor for hers. I also thank the many students at the University of East Anglia with whom I have enjoyed discussing Chaucer and the issues this book seeks to address. To my teachers, Derek Pearsall and the late Elizabeth Salter, my debts and thanks are boundless.

Acknowledgement is due to the Oxford University Press and to Houghton Mifflin for permission to quote from *The Works of Geoffrey Chaucer*, ed. F.N. Robinson (2nd edn, 1957).

1

Towards Reading Chaucer

This brief introduction to Chaucer's writing is necessarily highly selective. Necessarily, because the range of possible critical approaches is immense, and because the writer's work is very substantial, in every sense of that word. But while the book's brevity and approach make this stand out with rather startling plainness, processes of massive selectivity (in both critical paradigm and textual material) are involved in even the longest and most 'scholarly' work. It is best to be as open as possible about this. I have chosen to organise this book around the poet's exploration of a few major topics—'major' to Chaucer and of 'major' interest to many readers today. If the essays stimulate discussion of Chaucer's poetry, of the issues on which I concentrate and of the problematic, ideologically-loaded nature of reading, they will serve their purpose.

To begin with the obvious: like any human, Chaucer wrote from and for the specific historical contexts within which he lived. As our personal experience and identity is inextricably social, so the poet drew on language, ideas, practices and collective experiences which were given by the culture he inhabited. These contexts are not 'background' to the writing, a rather remote reference-point only of interest to historians. On the contrary, they are inscribed in the minute particulars of the texts: they permeate them, enable them, shape them. For texts, immersed in history, are social acts. Through them the world is mediated, prevalent perceptions are reinforced or challenged, contemporary values, experiences and problems represented, worked over. They are, indeed, made by actual people in living relationships, but made within determinate systems (social, political, linguistic, sexual, literary), and within circumstances they have not chosen. Any attempt to understand literature must include the attempt to re-place it in the web of discourses, social relations and practices where it was produced, the attempt to discover what problems, what questions it was addressing.

In trying to re-place texts in these webs we need to remember that surviving evidence about the medieval past—manorial, governmental, military, urban and other administrative records, as well as, for example, sermons, homilies and the writings we now classify as 'literature'—represents the dominant classes' version of significant reality. The loudest voices echoing across the centuries are those propagating the culture's dominant and officially sanctioned ideology. (By ideology I mean a system of concepts and images which constitute a way of seeing and interpreting the human world; a particular framework within which representation and evaluation take place. Ideologies construct versions of social reality and individual identity in accord with the general interests, power and assumptions of those social groups which sponsor them.) When the lives and views of the vast majority of people are refracted it is only as they impinge on the dominant classes' 'reality', and then the representation is through the highly partial ideological grid of these dominant groups. Nevertheless, we will listen carefully to these loud voices, and their representation of others' voices, since we need to reconstruct the culture's dominant ideology, its aspirations and its registration of pressures: this provides basic material in the composition of any text a critic will study. But while most surviving texts seek to enforce the dominant commonplaces, we must never define the period in the terms of its 'loudest' voices. The dominant ideology did not have as total a hold as we are often led to believe, and at least some surviving works were produced in an actively critical relation with it. The poetry discussed in this book is largely of this kind. It works over ruling ideas, conventional pieties and the unexamined norms of official culture in a way that subjects them to processes of criticism, processes which can include estrangement, distancing and even subversion. That some late medieval works manifest such processes in their treatment of received orthodoxies is hardly surprising. For European societies were far more diversified and dynamic than many literary critics assume.[1] The culture was far from homogeneous and many people wrote out of an acute and well-justified sense of ideological, institutional and social dislocation. Fourteenth-century historical processes were replete with conflicts and often extremely violent. As J.L. Bolton observes in his recent study of *The Medieval English Economy*, 'the research of the past three-quarters of a century has destroyed the idea of a uniform medieval society .... this was not a homogeneous society'. Indeed, from different perspectives, drawing on different evidence recent historical research shows how the fourteenth-century involved 'some of the most bitter and destructive class warfare to be seen in Europe before the Industrial Revolution'. The historian who wrote this, R.E. Lerner, goes on to comment: 'During that period of economic and political instability, men seldom found the traditional answers adequate to meet the crushing new problems that

3

seemed to arise on all sides.'[2] Despite some admirable exceptions (for example, Sheila Delany, Stephen Knight, Janet Coleman, see pp. 115–16) it is still true that these aspects of Chaucer's Europe are habitually obscured by commentators of the medieval texts selected and taught as 'literature' in our departments of 'Medieval Language and Literature'. This frees the field for critics to project myths about 'the medieval mind' and its age of homogeneous faith, harmonious order, unquestioned hierarchy and unchallenged authority, an age for which all problems could be solved by referring to the thirteenth-century *Summa* of St. Thomas Aquinas, if not to the still earlier work of St. Augustine. But the historical research 'of the past three-quarters of a century' should make it easier for students to recognise such literary-critical assumptions for the nostalgic projections they are, testifying more to modern critics' longings for a lost psychic unity than to any recognisable historical past.

Not, of course, that official religion and the cohesion it sought, was unimportant. The Church was a massively prominent presence. In various ways it affected everybody's life, most sharply in the ending of life and the fear of the after-life. It posed as the sole medium for God's saving grace, as the absolutely authoritative pronouncer of the correct view on everything—from the nature of God to the most intimate details of sexual relations; from the structure of the universe to the correct interpretation of those texts gathered together as the Bible, translated and kept in Latin under the control of its clerical caste. There was, so the Church proclaimed, no salvation outside its own institutional apparatus. This it figured as Noah's ark bearing the tiny minority of saved Christian souls through waters teeming with the mass of the eternally damned. Rejecting its authority was treated as a rejection of God, and if openly persisted in was punished with violent death (as some English Lollards witnessed in the fifteenth century)—and violent torture through eternity.[3] Yet this powerful religious institution, generating such grandiose self-images and self-justifications, was a vast vested interest, closely bound up with the medieval ruling classes, thoroughly incorporated in the contemporary social, economic and political fabric. This held true at all its levels, from the papal court to the clerical careerist to the poorest parish. The integration of the 'sacred' institution in the drives of the 'profane' world is nicely exemplified in a charge brought against a vicar for infringing the Statute of Labourers, the gentry's laws to keep down wages. The Church's official refused to perform the marriage service at traditional pre-plague prices and was accused of claiming what was seen as an extortionate fee—five or six shillings.[4] Reading Chaucer's very distinctive treatment of his Church and its 'sacred' officials we need to remember the severe contradictions between its self-representations and its contemporary existence, between accounts of Christ's poverty, teaching and actions in the Gospels and the practices of the late medieval Church. Chaucer's art engaged profoundly with such important contradictions, ones which perturbed many contemporary people, both orthodox and dissident.[5] We will return to Chaucer's mediations of this major context in Chapter 3.

Yet while historical exploration is an intrinsic part of reading and understanding, it involves deeper complications than the difficulties of reconstructing the relevant contexts. For all reconstruction is undertaken with a subjectivity shaped by the specific social world in and through which we have been able to develop our very consciousness and identity, let alone our habits of reading. The reader is a product of the cultural system within which she or he reads, however heterogeneous and differentiated this system may be. Even a rudimentary awareness of the metamorphosis texts undergo in changing cultures foregrounds the role of readers' assumptions and concerns in all interpretative activity. That the readers' horizons and cultural system should play such a part is inevitable, however seriously we undertake historical exploration. What is avoidable, however, is the all too common position in which teachers seek to present their own reading as quite free from ideology, free from any political dimensions, free from gender-based prejudices and orientation, indeed quite free from the determinations of historical living. This position merely camouflages the presence of the interpreter with his or her socially specific assumptions, interests and choices. Michel Foucault thinks conventional historians 'take unusual pains to erase the elements in their work which reveal their grounding in a particular time and place, their preferences in a controversy—the unavoidable obstacles of their passion': his observation applies as appropriately to most conventional scholars of medieval literature. We need to become as conscious as possible about the choices we make in our reading, our interpretation, our criticism: 'In any academic study we select the objects and methods of procedures which we believe the most important, and our assessment of their imporance is governed by frames of interest deeply rooted in our practical forms of social life.'[6] This formulation applies to the author of the present as of every other book. Its critical models inevitably carry specific political implications, prioritise certain issues rather than others, are more attentive to certain features than others. Readers will focus on and evaluate my reading through judgements informed by their own ideology. It should, however, be stressed that any adequate reading of medieval texts must hold to both critical moments described in this chapter, whatever the problems and however insurmountable the contradictions they may generate. That is, our reading needs to be informed by a serious attempt to reconstruct the text's moment of production, its own contexts of discourse and social practices within and for which it achieved meaning. Without this we risk a monumentally egotistic and finally tedious projection of our own being onto every other human product, however alien. While undertaking this essential historical attempt we must simultaneously acknowledge what has recently been described as 'the unavoidable given of all cognitive processes—that knowledge, however we may define it, is received through a situated human consciousness, that has spatiotemporal location, idiosyncratic colourations, and philosophical and sociopolitical prejudices.'[7] Our historical explorations are indeed mediated in these ways, for such is the fundamental structure, contingency and boundary of human knowing, the knowing of beings immersed in time, in specific cultural and social circumstances.

I shall conclude this chapter by illustrating Chaucer's own kind of fascination with the presence of the 'knower' and his or her interests in the 'known', the reader in the read. This fascination permeates his earlier poems, *The Book of the Duchess, The House of Fame, The Parliament of Fowls*.[8] It also emerges in his translation of Boethius's *Consolation of Philosophy*, where a recurrent source of intellectual error is said to be the failure to acknowledge the constitutive role of the knower in what is taken as known. Wrongly, people tend to assume

> that of alle the thingis that every wyght hath iknowe, thei wenen that tho thingis ben iknowe al only by the strenghte and by the nature of the thinges that ben iwyst or iknowe. And it is al the contrarye; for al that evere is iknowe, it is rather comprehendid and knowen, nat aftir his strengthe and his nature, but aftir the faculte (that is to seyn, the power and the nature) of hem that knowen. (Book V, *prosa* 4)

Texts, history, science, all we know is partially constituted by 'the power and nature' of the knower. While the model of the knower here is inadequately abstract, assuming, a desocialised, dehistoricised individual, it indicates a web of epistemological problems that Chaucer's work constantly engaged with.

Let us look briefly at an example of Chaucer's treatment of such issues in the *Nun's Priest's Tale*. This is one of Chaucer's most exuberant rhetorical displays. It works over a wide range of literary forms and styles (including the vocabulary of scholastic disputations), culminating in a joke whose target is the dominant form of official interpretative activity in his culture, moralising exegesis. Here comment is on only one aspect of this poem, its attention to interpretation and authoritative knowledge.

The poem's courtly cock, the 'gentil' Chauntecleer, and his wife, 'faire damoysele Pertelote', respond to a text, the husband's troubled dream written down at lines 2892–907. Madame Pertelote may be 'Curteys ... discreet and debonaire' but she makes a thoroughly materialist reading to debunk the male's solemnly supernaturalist interpretation (ll.2921–69). In her view, the text reveals the dreamer's physical disequilibrium which can be cured by very earthy means, a 'laxatyf': 'To purge yow bynethe and eek above', preceded by 'digestyves/Of wormes'. She offers to show her husband which herbs are effective, telling him in a language which eschews all courtly idiom: 'Pekke hem up right as they growe and ete hem yn.' Not content with this, she produces an 'authority' to support her sceptical approach to the interpretation of dreams—Cato (ll.2940–1). But the 'gentil cok' (l.2665) rejects both his wife's language and her disrespectful interpretation of his text. Choosing a mixture of courtly, homiletic and scholastic styles, he sets out to correct her misinterpretation. He puts forward a supernaturalistic reading, and grounds it in an appeal to the tradition of 'olde bookes' and allegedly impersonal, objective 'auctorite', a metaphysical tradition he claims to be decisively supported by 'experience'. So confident is he that he asserts:

> Ther nedeth make of this noon argument;
> The verray preeve sheweth it in dede.
>
> (ll.2982–3)

'Experience' is mediated through the grid of chosen 'auctorite', while 'auctorite' is deployed to end argument, to banish ambiguity and to organise 'experience' into the dominant, 'authoritative', system of knowledge which cannot itself be brought into question (ll.2970–83). Chaucer's text treats this standard aim of authoritative discourse as comically at odds with the real processes of interpretation and the genesis of human or hen-and-cock knowledge. Language and power are inextricably bound up.

For the 'gentil cok', a husband 'roial', has, like so many authoritative interpreters, overlooked a factor Chaucer's art constantly foregrounds—the shaping presence of the knower and his interests in construing what is known. Here, for example, the poem shows how the male's discourse includes the will to reassert authority over his wife and her materialist reading, one which so unflatteringly emphasises his own embodied nature, 'bynethe and eek above'. His long reply appeals to many a weighty 'auctorite', to 'ensamples olde', to saints' lives and to the male clerical caste's language, Latin, the language which, significantly, displaces the *mother*-tongue. This exhibits the self-congratulatory way jargon of a social group works against those outside it to keep them outside, the way, when the group is a privileged one, it serves the maintenance of power:

> *Mulier est hominis confusio*,—
> Madame, the sentence of this Latyn is,
> 'Womman is mannes joye and al his blis.
>
> (ll.3164–6)

Merely having access to an élite's language makes the male

speaker feel a very superior person, free to mock the Latin-less listener (see likewise the *Pardoner's Prologue*, ll.341-6). He refuses Pertelote any response, silencing her for the rest of the poem—a fine image of triumphant authority! We glimpse something of the way exegesis and conflicts over interpretation are bound up with the organisation of social and institutional *power* in the interpreter's situation.

Correspondingly, if the power structures are challenged or destabilised, the current nature of interpretation will be affected. As the text demonstrates, appeals to authority only serve their purpose while there is a consensus in the community about which texts should count as authority and about just how they should be read. This consensus enables people to ignore the fact that 'authority' is a contingent historical construct, shaped by specific social and economic relations with the structures of power they enable. But once the consensus breaks down, for whatever reasons, such naive interpretative approaches become unsatisfactory except for the most desperately authoritarian. The complex processes of interpretation are themselves presented as topics for critical reflection while the highly partial nature of authority and its deployment is made visible. (There seem to be links here with a movement in fourteenth-century philosophy which paid growing attention to the *conditions* and *limits* of knowledge at the expense of traditional systematic metaphysics and natural theology.[9]) Like *The House of Fame*, the *Nun's Priest's Tale* depicts a situation where the appeal to authority, far from closing an issue, threatens to open out an interpretative abyss. The female's appeal to authority is met by the male's assertion that *his* appeal is to 'many a man moore of auctorite' than hers, all of whom give 'the revers' of her view (ll.2970-7). But by what criteria are interpreters to select between radically contradictory authorities? The comedy lays bare the unselfconscious arrogance in all assumptions that humans have access to a totally objective, impersonal viewpoint from which interpretative conflicts can be subjected to a final judgement. Such a perspective could only be attributed to a transcendental reader—that is, a non-human one.

In this poem the struggle over interpretation ends with the male dismissing the topic and displaying the machismo which has been part of his competitive wish to subdue the woman in argument. He moves from the textual to the sexual with relief and pride:

> He fethered Pertelote twenty tyme,
> And trad hire eke as ofte, er it was pryme.
> He looketh as it were a grym leoun,
> And on his toos he rometh up and doun;
> Hym deigned nat to sette his foot to grounde.
> . . .
> Thus roial, as a prince is in his halle. . .
> (ll.3177–81, 3184)

The text yokes the male will to dominate in an overtly 'intellectual' sphere with the current forms of sexual organisation and a discourse saturated with male domination (see Chapter 4), but it does not pursue this topic. Nevertheless, even hints at this issue, taken up most cogently in the *Wife of Bath's Prologue* (ll.693–710), enforce the poem's subversion of all approaches which would render the nature of authority unproblematic and assume that interpretation can be perfectly objective and impersonal.

At its close the *Nun's Priest's Tale* redirects its preoccupation with interpretation towards itself and its readers. They may well expect a conventional moralisation of the fable, in the manner of Robert Henryson's own version of Chaucer's story, the 'Taill of Schir Chanteclair and the Foxe'. Here Henryson attaches a '*moralitas*', outlining a series of banal propositions about the dangers of

11

pride and flattery.[10] Such moralising, when in earnest, involves a kind of textual policing, a wish to *control* both the text and the reader's imaginative intelligence, to ensure they keep within currently orthodox versions of reality, truth and moral righteousness. Many 'scholarly' readings of the *Nun's Priest's Tale* do, indeed, provide the work with a simple 'moralite': sometimes of Henryson's kind, sometimes more pietistic, with the fox representing the devil or false friars, the cock the Christian soul or the secular clergy, the old dairymaid, Holy Church...Chaucer, however, foresaw such readerly nostalgia for a stable, unquestionable authority—he had, after all, enough experience of it in his own culture and its most prevalent exegetical practices.[11] So he placed it in his own poem's ending. He allows the reader to collapse his multifaceted tale into homiletic banality:

> Lo, swich it is for to be recchelees
> And necligent, and truste on flaterye.
> (ll.3436–7)

Then he considers the reader who needs the reassurance of an allegorical grid to impose unambiguous law and order on the dynamic text:

> But ye that holden this tale a folye,
> As of a fox, or of a cok and hen,
> Taketh the moralite, goode men.
> For seint Paul seith that al that writen is,
> To our doctrine it is ywrite, ywis;
> Taketh the fruyt, and lat the chaf be stille.
> (ll.3438–43)

The joke here is against those who feel the pressure to abstract an authoritative 'moralite': they do so because they quite overlook the poem's hermeneutic explorations, finding only 'a folye' about animals. It is also against those who in the light shed by this poem could find the claim that everything written is written 'To our doctrine' anything other than a naive evasion of all the most fundamental problems in interpretation. In the same way, the text is simply dissolved by those who, at its close, take the metaphor of 'fruyt' and 'chaf' in the unproblematic way it was habitually used by clerical exegetes describing their own allegorical practices. By whose criteria will such evaluative distinctions between 'fruyt' and 'chaf' be made, in whose interests, to what purposes? The poem could, in fact, only be brought under the control of an allegorist's authoritative grid by extreme interpretative violence. For a playful but thoroughly critical reflection on the processes by which such grids are constructed is one of the poem's characteristics. It is characteristic of more in Chaucer's writing than the *Nun's Priest's Tale.*

2

Chaucer's Representations of Society

Society was traditionally and authoritatively represented as a body organised in three estates: massive differences in power, access to resources, and status were allegedly in everyone's interest, the 'common profit'. Those who worked to sustain the basic life processes of the community (the lowest estate), those who were said to defend (= police?) the community (the knightly estate), and those who prayed (the clerical estate, bringing the community and God together), comprised the static, harmonious organism created by God. In it, all individuals should unquestioningly accept their inherited occupation and place. This dominant social ideology generated a mass of writings encouraging people to see themselves according to some version of its basic model and the values it carried. These writings presented the established division of power, wealth, work and knowledge as so 'natural' that any opposition to it must seem 'unnatural', monstrous.[1] This is, of course, always one of the chief functions of social ideology sponsored by dominant classes. Human identity becomes defined in its terms—

14

'There be in þis world þre maner of men, clerkes, knyʒtes, and commynalte.'[2]

However, as indicated in the opening chapter, this ideology faced substantial anomalies by Chaucer's time, and well before then, in fact. Increasing social complexity, emerging social groups (especially with the great urban developments of the thirteenth-century), sharp social conflicts, the development of a profit economy, diversification of political theory and even the articulation of competing ideologies, constituted a world intractable to received frames of reference. Chaucer's writing is marked by an openness to many of the contradictory forces in this fluid situation.

About the time of the great, popular English rising of 1381, Chaucer wrote the *Parliament of Fowls*, a multifaceted, energetic poem which includes a representation of society and social ideologies. In this poem Nature, a personified metaphysical concept, supports a traditional perception of the community as a stable hierarchy. In isolation, this would look like the traditional authoritarian move whereby existing social order is made 'natural' and hence unquestionable, eternal. But the text offers us, against this, a figuration of conflict and violently egotistical behaviour, with each competing group presenting its own views as disinterested concern for 'commune profyt'. The leading groups are named first in a pointed manner:

> That is to seyn, the foules of ravyne
> Weere hyest set, and thanne the foules smale
> . . .
> Ther was the tiraunt with his fetheres donne
> And grey, I mene the goshauk, that doth pyne
> To bryddes for his outrageous ravyne.
> (ll.323-4, 334-6)

The dominant and powerful are thus presented as predators,

tyrants and perpetrators of 'outrageous ravyne' (1.340). Through his explicitly social categories (the birds' language, the political form of a parliament), the poet invites the reader to take this as a gamesome model of the society she or he inhabits. The aristocratic birds, speaking a distinctly courtly language, monopolise the assembly (ll.414–90) and make the needs of other groups in the community quite invisible, literally unspeakable. Talk of common profit from such emphatically class-bound leaders is made rather ironic. Nor, significantly, are the lower orders, the creatures of the third estate, at all impressed. Instead of deferential respect, they burst into a very different language from the courtly figures, one expressing direct antagonism to the upper classes. The text creates conflicting forms of social life which involve conflicting perspectives and values:

> . . .'Have don, and lat us wende!'
> . . .
> 'Com of!' they criede, 'allas, ye wol us shende!
> Whan shal youre cursede pletynge have an ende?
> . . .
> The goos seyde, 'Al this nys not worth a flye!. . .'
>
> (ll.492, 494–5, 501)

This explosion challenges the upper-class monopoly of Parliament, power and speech. It works as a characteristically Chaucerian image of what Rodney Hilton has described as, 'The loss of plebeian respect for the traditional élites' in this period, an image of social energies recreated in a very different mode by Chaucer's contemporary, Langland.[3] Not that the privileged Chaucer saw the lower social groups as carrying more admirable values. He has the lower-status cuckoo invoke the notion of common welfare only to disclose that here too self-interest underlies the rhetoric of charitable intervention (ll.505–8, 605–6). His poem displays competing versions of what is 'commune profyt' in a complex and divided society such as his own. It unveils the highly partial perspectives informing the language of 'common welfare' and 'unity', while it blocks off any attempt to escape to some transcendental solution.

A similar approach to his social world and its language is evident in *The Canterbury Tales*. Its recognition should be prominent in our readings of that fragmentary, carnivalesque and unfinished work. The *General Prologue* alludes to traditional ideology of the three estates through the figures of Knight, Priest and Ploughman-Peasant. But it does so in a context which dissolves the estates ideology, within a literary form well suited to figure forth a mobile, dissonant social world penetrated by market values and pursuits—very familiar to its author, a wealthy vintner's son who spent his life in a major urban economy, moving as easily with wealthy bourgeoisie as with courtiers and urban intellectuals. Chaucer represents this society in a manner which encourages critical reflection on the relations between its official ideology, languages and practices, while discouraging simple traditional judgements. It is a mode which could help us take a striking question in the *General Prologue* as far more than a jibe at the Monk: 'How shal the world be served?' (l.187). In the poem's representation of social being this becomes deeply problematic.

Here, there is only space to illustrate this mode in the *General Prologue* by taking one figure, the Monk (ll.165–207). Jill Mann has described the way Chaucer evokes traditional stereotypes of the corrupt monk only to refine the conventional judgements these carried.[4] Certainly, the Monk is allowed to dismiss traditional rules and their attempts to confine monks to monastic cells:

> Ther as this lord was kepere of the celle,
> The reule of seint Maure or of seint Beneit,

17

> By cause that it was old and somdel streit
> This ilke Monk leet olde thynges pace,
> And heeld after the newe world the space.
>
> (ll.172–6)

Monks, like Chaucer, *did* inhabit 'the newe world', and the forces of 'the newe world' shaped religious practices and individual consciousness. As for the old proverbs asserting that monks out of their cloisters were like fish out of water:

> thilke text heeld he nat worth an oystre;
> And I seyde his opinion was good.
>
> (ll.182–3)

Readers should not take the assent here as simple sarcasm, whether they attribute it to Chaucer or the fictional pilgrim-narrator on whom so many words have been bestowed. For 'thilke text' had long since been made a dead letter, not by a few deviant, 'bad' monks, but by the development of monasticism within medieval society and its economy. The same applies to the comments that the Monk was an 'outridere', 'a lord ful fat' enjoying an aristocratic life-style, a 'manly man' and hence ideal for promotion within the religious establishment to the post of abbot (ll.166–71, 190–1, 200, 203–6). Monks, and especially their leaders, were drawn from the upper and middle classes, while the expansion of monasticism had been inextricably bound up with its economic foundations, practices and wordly success as a powerful landlord producing for medieval markets.[5] Chaucer's art engages with this situation. Instead of writing a satire which lampoons 'wordly' monks as individual deviants from an unquestionable moral order, it discloses traditional ideology as made anachronistic by the practices and new language of thriving Christian institutions in 'the newe world'. The poetry figures decisive social forces which shaped contemporary and future human practices in directions quite alien to received ideology and the estates satire this sponsored. We are shown some of the implications of the monastic economy which the historian Lester Little recently described in these terms:

> They [the Cistercians] did not slip casually into the profit economy, as had the black monks before them; instead—even if for the most part unintentionally—they plunged headlong into it. Their staying so far away from towns and their brilliant economic success together indicated how thoroughly the profit economy had permeated the countryside.[6]

In such circumstances the reiteration of traditional rules and moral outrage (perhaps congruent with an earlier feudal order?) was, Chaucer's art suggests, rather shallow. By his time, there was nothing 'unintentional' about monks' economic commitments.

Throughout the *General Prologue* we encounter a world in which moral vocabulary and judgements become terms to depict success and respectability in a world where the market is central. The Wife of Bath, a successful 'clooth-makyng' member of the bourgeoisie, is called 'a worthy womman' (ll.447,459); the Merchant, necessarily concentrating on 'th'encrees of his wynnyng' and representing the bourgeois life preoccupied with the market, its values and financial dealing, is called, 'a worthy man' (ll.274-9); the Knight fights 'in his lordes werre', but as he fights for both officially Christian employers and heathens he too seems a 'worthy man' in the sense that he is a successful operator in the same social world and discourse as the other pilgrims (11.42-72).[7] In these and similar cases it is a crude misreading to assume that 'really' Chaucer is being sarcastic at the expense of his 'persona', the fictional narrator mentioned above. Such misreading assumes that the text invites simple moral condemnation from a simply anti-mercantile position. Nobody had been more severely treated by traditional pre-capitalist moralists than the merchant. The thirteenth-century theologian, St Thomas Aquinas, was conventional enough when he asserted that 'trade, in so far as it aims at making profits, is most reprehensible, since the desire for gain knows no bounds but reaches the infinite.'[8] But the art of the London tradesman's son encourages no such moralisation. Rather, as Jill Mann has shown, the *General Prologue* stresses how 'worth' is defined according to professional criteria; it withholds any sense of that benevolent and organic interaction of estates so central in traditional social ideology. Chaucer's poetry dramatises the way a market society dissolves such traditional ideology and its ethical discourses while it shapes human relationships around the exchange of commodities. His work evokes human agents for whom traditional ideas of community and common profit are irrelevant anachronisms. The world emerging in the fiction is not unrelated to the 'newe world' Chaucer inhabited, one experiencing the substantial activity of mercantile capital and the historical consequences this held for human consciousness and relations.

* * *

Let us consider one of the less discussed *Canterbury Tales*—the *Shipman's Tale*. Like so many others of the tales, this plunges us into a world in which market relations are the norm. Marriage, marital sex, extramarital sex, all are for sale, all absorbed into the cash nexus. This state of affairs is encapsulated in the final pun on 'taille' in the wife's comment, 'score it up upon my taille'—genitals are account-books, sex is a commodity, marital sex the balancing of financial accounts. As the Wife of Bath is made to show, 'al is for to selle' (Wife of Bath's *Prologue*, l.414). These are matters returned to in the final chapter: here I wish to point out some of the more subtle ways in which Chaucer's text shows a market society affecting language, values and historical development. As in the *General Prologue*, words which are major terms in moral discourse become terms merely reflecting position and purchasing power in the economic market: 'wys' is a measure of 'wealth'; 'wys' human activity is defined as successful transactions on the international market, as is 'prudent' activity (*Shipman's Tale*, ll.2, 365-8, 64). Similarly, the key word 'good' loses any peculiarly ethical import and becomes a counter for signifying material possessions and their conventional value (ll.79-81, 243). Again, as in the *General Prologue*, 'worthy' takes on a purely professional and economistic frame of reference; so does the word for generosity, 'free' (ll.20, 43). It is also striking that the word 'noble' is applied to success in the market, something Gower observed and complained about in his *Miroir de l'omme*. There he asserted that, by the 1370s, 'the chivalric aristocracy is being replaced by a financial aristocracy: knights have become greedy for money, now fight only for ransom (MO, 23,695) and engage in trade rather than seeking military prowess (MO, 23,713).'[9] Similarly, in *Vox Clamantis*, he complained that, 'Arms are more of a business now than a mark of nobility, as a result, the tailor's boy now goes about in a helmet.'[10]

Chaucer himself represents the merchant's life as one quite uninhibited by any sense of the traditional religious guilt about this vocation. It is shown as founded on an utterly individualistic pursuit of wealth through market transactions in which rational calculation and credit is a key to success. What becomes of traditional Catholic Christianity in such a way of life? Chaucer's text includes an astonishingly resonant answer. During the visit of the merchant's friend, the monk, the host withdraws from the festivities:

21

> The thridde day, this marchant up ariseth,
> And on his nedes sadly hym avyseth,
> And up into his countour-hous gooth he
> To rekene with hymself, as wel may be,
> Of thilke yeer how that it with hym stood,
> And how that he despended hadde his good,
> And if that he encressed were or noon.
> His bookes and his bagges many oon
> He leith biforn hym on his countyng-bord.
> Ful riche was his tresor and his hord,
> For which ful faste his countour-dore he shette;
> And eek he nolde that no man sholde hym lette
> Of his acountes, for the meene tyme;
>
> (ll.75–87)

As this merchant 'up ariseth' on 'the third day' the religious and moral *potential* of this passage should be registered. For example, the potential echo of Christ's resurrection on the third day, with its traditional moral allegorisation as the rising from sin demanded of all people in Christianity; the traditional religious and ethical potential of the emphatically solitary ascent into an upper room for scrupulous introspection and meditation ('To rekene with himself, as wel may be. . .how that it with hym stood' and with his 'good'). Once we register this religious and ethical potential, we are well placed to understand the significance of the fact that far from being actualised the potential is stunningly transformed. For what Chaucer figures here is the way that such mercantile dedication to the market involves a psychological state which transforms traditional religious orientations in a manner that can be described as worldly asceticism.[11] This impression is strengthened by the juxtaposition of the merchant's solitary withdrawal on the third day with the monk's gregarious and festive presence in the worthy house. The merchant's retreat replaces the traditional retreat of monasticism, and with this, of course, the old goals. Instead of the monastic cell, the *counting house*; instead of the Bible and saints' lives, *accounting books*; instead of monastic withdrawal to undertake scrupulous introspection in the pursuit of the love of God and the heavenly treasures of supernatural salvation, the merchant withdraws from the festivities to undertake meticulous, systematic calculations in the pursuit of monetary profit and the accumulation of very material '*good*' and '*tresor*'. Nor is his daily practice unaffected by this withdrawal. We find him travelling to Flanders and working in Bruges,

> faste and bisily
> Aboute his nede, and byeth and creaunceth.
> He neither pleyeth at the dees ne daunceth...
> (ll.302–4)

As his business succeeds, he thanks God who has apparently graced his buying and selling (ll.344–5). Religion thus sanctifies a life centred on the individualistic and socially irresponsible pursuit of economic profit while the social milieu allows this, favours it, and even seems to take it for granted.

What then of the representative of the traditional pursuit of holiness, 'daun John' the monk? Like the Monk of the *General Prologue*, he has come out of his cell and into the world as an 'officer' licensed by his abbot to pursue the economic interests of his monastery, 'To seen hir graunges and hire bernes wyde' and to engage in market transactions to support the material foundations of a traditional religious order (ll.62 ff., 270ff.; GP*r*, ll.165–207). Chaucer displays the contradictions between the original spiritual basis of monastic vocation and its social, economic and religious outcome, a matrix referred to earlier in this chapter. In contrast to the merchant, the business monk is quite free of ascetic tendencies. Like the Monk of the *General Prologue*, he enjoys the traditional pleasures of the landed upper classes with a relish which Chaucer's poetry conveys in a manner and context which leaves little space or language for' traditional moral judgement.

In summary, then, Chaucer's work represents society as a composite of *inevitably* competing groups motivated by individualistic forms of material self-interest, and mediated through access to a market which he saw as encompassing and profoundly affecting most human relationships. In this vision all claims to be pursuing an allegedly *common profit* are exposed to a sceptical examination which subverts the very notion of a unified society and a harmonious common profit. With this goes a critical reflexivity which de-sublimates all attempts to erect ideologically secure, impersonally authoritative discourses. His texts continually return such discourses to the social processes within which they are generated and to which they contribute. Contrary to the dominant ideology, his work represents long-term *antagonism* between social groups as an altogether predictable, even inevitable state of affairs, while the literary modes he constructs subvert attempts to impose traditional social ideology and moralisations on what is exhibited as intractable material.

* * *

I shall now turn to the figuration of lordship, institutionalised secular authority, in two of Chaucer's most widely-read poems, the *Knight's Tale* and the *Clerk's Tale*. Contrary to much academic wisdom, which seems to have enlightened our sixth forms, the *Knight's Tale* is not an unequivocal celebration of Theseus as the principle of law and order we are to worship. It is a critical, often highly ironic, exploration of secular rule, its forms of power and its uses of language.

Theseus represents the successful 'lord and governour' (l.81), a 'worthy duc' (l.1001). The *General Prologue*, as we saw, shows what words like 'worthy' signify in the current culture of discourse, and by its usage here we understand that Theseus is an expert ruler, remembering how the Merchant, the Wife of Bath and the Friar are also all 'worthy' professionals.[12] What kind of order such 'worthy' and heroic military rulers propagate is made a major topic for reflection in the poem.

As soon as Chaucer introduces Theseus he makes the basis of his government clear—military domination (ll.860-5). His 'wysdom and his chivalrie' are concentrated on wars of imperialist expansion which have an explicit economic motive: 'riche' countries are violently conquered to feed Theseus's 'wele' and his 'pride' (ll.864, 895). The poem's opening thus displays the foundation of the honour and aristocratic life so celebrated in conventional romance literature. It also emphasises that Theseus is a worshipper of Mars (ll.975-6). The implications of this are drawn out in an extremely powerful passage, the depiction of Mars' temple and the ways of life pursued by that god's worshippers (ll.1967-2050). The writing here evokes the human misery produced by violent aggression and it works in a manner whose critical bearings are not widely appreciated. The text displays the *common ground* between the 'tiraunt with the pray by force yraft', leaving the 'toun destroyed', and the 'tresoun of the mordrynge in the bedde'; between the 'open werre' with masses 'slayn', the organised violence initiated by national rulers and the 'smylere with the knyf under the cloke'. The poetry persuades us to see *continuities* between supposedly different forms of violence. The ruling classes, however, strive to distinguish their own violence, which they glorify and aestheticise, from the violence of others, which they condem. Contemporary Anglo-American scholars have tended to overlook the critical dimension of the *Knight's Tale* here. Yet even orthodox Christians have not always been blind to the disturbing continuities the text depicts. St

Augustine himself likened the order of kingdoms to that of robber bands, asserting that the only difference between them is the impunity of official rulers.[13] Nor should we overlook the fact that having presented Theseus as the most successful conqueror of his era, riding under the banner of Mars, Chaucer now includes the image of 'Conquest, sittynge in greet honour' in this grisly temple of dehumanising violence (l.2028). The passage concludes with another allusion to Theseus's Martian banner where the 'rede statue of Mars' shone in glory. Now the 'statue of Mars' is more closely described. We learn that the god Theseus worships seems insane (l.2042), while

> A wolf ther stood biforn hym at his feet
> With eyen rede, and of a man he eet;
> (ll.2047–8)

Such is the 'glorie' of Mars (l.2050) and his followers critically placed by Chaucer. The passage justly conveys the destructive contempt for humanity in the forms of law, order and life cultivated by rulers who exalt armed 'force', 'glorie' and 'honour'.

Given this, it should not be surprising that the poem shows how, when rulers of armed states accuse each other of tyranny, the accusations tend to lack political self-awareness even if they are not—as they mostly are—cynical propaganda. In the *Knight's Tale* Creon is accused of 'tirannye' and Theseus promises to ride out as a 'trewe knyght' to smash this tyrant (ll. 941, 959–61). But the poem conveys the self-interest and self-aggrandising motives in this righteousness (ll.905–8, 962–3). It follows Theseus's liberation of Thebes from the tyranny of Creon by giving us another decisive insight to the form of law and order the 'worthy' duke represents. Having killed Creon, he assaults Thebes, 'And rente adoune bothe wall and sparre and rafter' (l.990). This act of wanton violent destruction is a 'worthy' one for a follower of Mars in whose temple the destruction of civilian homes is figured (l.2016). After this, Theseus 'dide with al the contree as hym leste' (l.1004). Palamon's complaint about Theseus's 'tirannye' (l.1111) is not at all foolish. Indeed, at this point Chaucer adds a passage not in his Italian source to bring out still more sharply the implications of law and order as understood by the world's Theseuses:

> To ransake in the taas of bodyes dede,
> Hem for to strepe of harneys and of wede,
> The pilours diden bisynesse and cure
> After the bataille and disconfiture.
>
> (ll.1005–8)

The scene takes us to the core of militaristic cultures, just as it focuses on the essential economic groundwork—ground so assiduously obscured by official pomp, pageantry and glorifications of war. The mentality which fosters any form of militarism culminates in an easy willingness to turn the vitally alive into dead bodies, ransacked for the victors' economic profit and their rulers' 'mooste pride' (l.895). The passage creates a memorable image of cultures which transform humans into objects, things, profitable dead things.

Some readers take Theseus's organisation of the tournament in which Arcite is killed as a sign of benevolent rule. Yet the poem hardly encourages a totally unironic response. True enough, the ruler does separate Palamon and Arcite, those emblems of a 'chivalrie' whose knightly ideals turn them into forms of life depicted in animal images such as 'wood leon', 'crueel tigre' and 'wilde bores' that 'frothen white as foom' (ll.1649–60). But Theseus controls them because they threaten his lordship, his own monopoly over the means and deployment of violence (ll.1704–13). As soon as he hears who they are, he announces that he need not torture the Thebans but can kill them immediately, 'by mighty Mars the rede' (l.1747). The courtly ladies intervene successfully at this point and Theseus relents. Nevertheless, his 'pitee' is still quite explicitly part of a political calculation (ll.1821–34). It is also a peculiarly Martian version of 'pitee'. He could, after all, have settled the question of who, if anyone, should marry Emily in a host of non-violent ways—heresy of heresies, he could even have followed the lead of Nature in the *Parliament of Fowls* and allowed the female some choice (ll.407–13, 627–8)! Instead, he centralises and increases the violence by ordering each of the two Thebans to bring another hundred armed knights who will fight until one of the leaders is killed or defeated (ll.1845–61). Later, Theseus does decide to limit the instruments of violence to lances, long swords and maces to protect the shedding of 'gentil blood', the blood of his own class (ll.2537–60). However, he still exhorts the armed knights to 'ley on faste', to fight their fill (ll.2549, 2558–9). The text then depicts the ensuing violence as bloody and animalistic (ll.2601–35). Simultaneously, in a profoundly illuminating juxtaposition, it shows the ruler who has organised the dehumanising violence surveying the scene as a spectacle while he sits above it, 'Arrayed right as he were a god in trone' (l.2529). Such is still the custom of the lords of violence. As for the tournament, after the intervention of the culture's appropriately vicious gods, it ends in the miserable death of Arcite described in a mode which decisively resists all idealisation and glorification (ll.2742–79).

With this in mind it is worth recalling Chaucer's *Tale of Melibee*. This includes a critique of conventional 'machismo' and upper-class aggression (*Melibee*, ll.1018 ff., 1034 ff., 1285–94). It argues that war should not be glorified and must be avoided (ll.1664 ff., 1679 ff.), stressing 'the grete goodes that comen of pees, and the grete harmes and perils that been in werre' (l.1728). The work, itself conventional enough, is a salutary check on certain current myths about what 'the medieval mind' must have thought about war. With it one does well to recall the writing of Chaucer's close friend, the Lollard knight, John Clanvowe. In his treatise on *The two ways* he remarks that conventional defence and glorification of war may be antithetical to God's judgements, for unlike God:

> þe world [his class?] holt hem worsshipful þat been greet werreyours and fiʒteres and þat distroyen and wynnen manye loondis, and waasten and ʒeuen muche good to hem þat haan ynouʒ. And also þe world worsshipeþ hem muchel þat woln bee venged proudly and dispitously of euery wrong þat is seid or doon to hem. And of swyche folke men maken bookes and soonges and reeden and syngen of hem for to hoolde þe mynde of here deedes þe lengere heere vpon eerth.

Clanvowe, however, insists that 'God is souuerayn treuþe and a trewe iuge þat deemeth hem riʒt shameful byfore God and alle þe compaigne of heuene'.[14] The lucidity with which he identifies and condemns the ideological dimensions of romance is striking, setting himself (and his God, of course) in opposition to a matrix in which practice and discourse are inseparable. Chaucer's *Melibee* and his friend's tract offer a medieval perspecitve too often ignored. It is far closer to the informing critical vision of the *Knight's Tale* than those perpetuated by the commentaries emerging from the Anglo-American community of 'medievalists' which make the poem a hymn in honour of Theseus and his values.

The *Knight's Tale* concludes with a long parliamentary oration in which Theseus seeks specific *political* gains. The text is quite unequivocal about this:

> Thanne semed me ther was a parlement
> At Atthenes, upon certain pointz and caas;

> Among the whiche pointz yspoken was,
> To have with certein contrees alliaunce,
> And have fully of Thebans obeisaunce.
> For which this noble Theseus anon
> Leet senden after gentil Palamon
>
> (ll.2970–6)

Theseus's motivation is plainly political self-interest perceived through that will for dominion which becomes so basic to those leading a society's ruling class. (Indeed, the speech is explicitly an expression of the ruler's 'wille' [l.2986].) Here the leader and his Parliament determine a foreign policy which includes total control of those whose city they had earlier destroyed, tearing down 'bothe wall and sparre and rafter' (l.990). Through the speech itself, Chaucer shows how theological language can serve those in power. It enables them to present thoroughly limited class and nationalistic self-interests as universal ones dictated by a transcendental being to whom they have special, indeed monopolistic, access. Wonderful to say, this being never criticises the basic activities or views of the ruling class and never, never supports its opponents! Chaucer has sharpened the irony in this political oration by having the very worldly, militaristic Theseus, whose speech culminates in an order for a very wordly, wealthy and merry upper-class marriage, plunder bits and pieces from one of the poet's favourite texts, the *Consolation of Philosopy*. Boethius wrote this as part of an attempt to cultivate stoical detachment from the kind of world to which Theseus is so totally devoted: and he did so while awaiting execution decreed by his own worthy ruler.

Not suprisingly, Theseus transforms the *Consolation of Philosophy* into a *Consolation of Political Authority*. His oration, purportedly a rhetorical elaboration of the banal observation that all things must die, actually aims to persuade us that whatever is, is right. Indeed, the present social order is naturalised, eternalised and given divine rather than human and historical foundations. Theseus's message is one we have become accustomed to hearing from our political leaders who represent the chief beneficiaries of the social and economic order which sustains them:

> Thanne is it wysdom, as it thynketh me,
> To maken vertu of necessitee,
> And take it weel that we may nat eschue,
> And namely that to us alle is due.
> And whoso gruccheth ought, he dooth folye,
> And rebel is to hym that al may gye.
>
> (ll.3041–6)

This is a highly partial and impoverished idea of human 'wysdom', but its political uses are hardly obscure. The discourse of authority would persuade us that its truncated version of reality is definitive. The slightest complaint against the current order is construed as madness, a madness which turns the protestor into a 'rebel' against God with whom the secular powers and their order are now conveniently merged. This is the context in which he pronounces it wisdom 'To maken vertu of necessitee', a context in which his own rule and its contingent social order are claimed as 'necessitee'. Richard Neuse is right to remind us how Milton placed such language in *Paradise Lost*:

> So spoke the Fiend, and with necessity,
> The tyrant's plea, excused his devilish deeds,
>
> (Book IV, ll.393–4)[15]

The meaning of 'love' in the speech undergoes as characteristic a reduction as 'wysdom'. It becomes a merely controlling and limiting force supporting the present order and its ruler (ll.2987–93, 3011–40). All elements in the oration converge in a sacralisation of Theseus's secular authority. We now see the full meaning of Theseus presenting himself 'as he were a god in trone' (1.2529)—visual image, state pageantry, theology and the language of political control fuse. It is salutary to remember that for such sacralisation of his own authority, King Richard II, was finally deposed and killed by the man Chaucer lauded as 'verray kyng'.[16]

* * *

The *Clerk's Tale* is my second example of Chaucer's treatment of lordship. The critical power of this poem has been too often obscured by medievalists who seem to identify with Walter.[17] This would hardly have surprised Chaucer, for he anticipated the likelihood of absolutist misreadings, mockingly placing them in the mouths of the Host and the Merchant. He also acknowledges that 'som men' will praise Walter's subjection of Griselda, but has the narrator make his own condemnation of such readers quite unequivocal (ll.456–62, 622–3).

In fact, the text's condemnation of Walter could not be more direct. His actions are described as evil ('wikke', ll.785–6) and his purpose as 'crueel' (ll.734, 740). Walter is presented as a lawful ruler consumed by an insatiable lust for absolute dominion. Indeed, the word most frequently associated with him, from the opening description of him as one for whom 'his lust present was al his thoght', is the word 'lust' (ll.80, 105, 111, 322, 351–4, 531, 619, 647, 660, 662, 716–17, 758). His statement to Griselda's father illustrates assumptions about lordship common enough among authoritarian rulers: 'al that liketh me, I dar wel seyen/It liketh thee' (ll.311–12). It is the ideal he proposes to Griselda:

I seye this, be ye redy with good herte
To al my lust, and that I frely may,
As me best thynketh, do yow laughe or smerte,
And nevere ye to grucche it, nyght ne day?
And eek whan I sey 'ye', ne sey nat 'nay',
Neither by word ne frownyng contenance?
Sware this, and heere I swere oure alliance.

(ll.351-7)

This is the ideal of all tyrants, whether domestic, in the world of work, or in the formally political sphere. Just as Theseus claimed that 'whoso *gruccheth* ought, he dooth folye,/And rebel is', so Walter demands that his subject never 'grucche it'. While her father stood before Walter 'al quakyng', so Griselda listens 'quakynge for drede'. Not suprisingly, she assents (l.317, 358-64). This is a disturbing image of authority and obedience—nor is it one cherished by many late medieval people in practice or theory.

From here the poem displays the effects of such a political relation (for 'personal' relations are also 'political', and vice versa). The lord indulges in a rule of absolute and totally irresponsible sovereignty, driven on by a compulsive will over which he is shown to have no control (ll.453-8, 617-23, 696-707, 732-5, 785-7). He becomes an example of a man overwhelmed by what St Augustine had called 'the love of ruling' which 'lays waste men's hearts with the most ruthless dominion'.[18] But it is not only the ruler's moral state that is perverted in such a relation. The moral life of the obedient subject is also corrupted. Chaucer depicts this through the sergeant. Committed to 'feithful' service and unquestioning obedience, 'swich folk', the poet writes, will carry out 'thynges badde' if they are ordered to (ll.319-22). The sergeant's view is that men *must* obey their rulers' 'lust', 'ther is namoore to seye' (ll.526-32). This is the subject's version of Theseus's instruction to suspend all critical reflection or

33

dissent, to accept the existing state of affairs as 'necessitee' and to make a 'vertu' of capitulation to it. (Such ideas did not offer any protection for the followers of Richard II executed in 1388.) Griselda's attitude is no different from the sergeant's, and no less culpable. In her servile obedience to her ruler, she renounces all responsibility, moral or religious. The terrible consequences of such subjection are made clear. It actually encourages vicious tyranny and it leads the subject into unambiguously evil actions. Griselda assents to the murder of her children without any attempt to protect them and without any protest or attempt to reform her vicious lord. Theseus's or Walter's ideal subject, she accepts the authoritarian ruler's self-deification, an acceptance the text treats with critical penetration. The deification of a 'cruel' and 'wikke' secular order is, if we wish to use theological terms, idolatry.[19]

The poem is thus a powerful dramatisation of the effects of absolutism on both the ruled and the ruler. Its meaning should also be viewed in its own contexts—the contexts of Richard II's reign with its sharp and, for some, fatal, political and ideological conflicts. In these the distinction between legitimate rule and arbitrary absolutism, or tyranny, had become a live issue which Chaucer knew and experienced at first hand.[20] These conflicts were only to be resolved with the overthrow of Richard. This was chiefly justified in the 1399 Articles of Deposition on the grounds that the ruler had become a tyrant exercising arbitrary will in the mistaken assumption that law resided in his own breast. He had, that is to say, become a Walter. But his Griselda rebelled.[21]

Chaucer's text does include an alternative, if rather abstractly idealistic model of political authority to Walter's, and we should not overlook it. In Walter's absence Griselda becomes ruler. Her renunciation of the lust for power enables her to mediate between competing and conflicting groups, introducing judgements not of arbitrary will but of 'greet equitee'. She thus earns the trust and voluntary cooperation of the community (ll.430–41). This is presented as an ideal and contrasts starkly with Walter's practices, as with all the absolutist ideologies he represents. It certainly matches the model expressed in Chaucer's *Legend of Good Women*:

> This shulde a ryghtwys lord han in his thought,
> And not ben lyk tyraunts of Lumbardye,
> That usen wilfulhed and tyrannye.
> For he that kyng or lord is naturel,
> Hym oughte nat be tyraunt and crewel,
> As is a fermour, to don the harm he can.
> He moste thynke it is his lige man
> And that hym oweth, of verrary duetee,
> Shewen his peple pleyn benygnete,
> And wel to heren here excusacyouns.
> And here compleyntes and petyciouns
>
> (*Prologue*, G, ll.353–63)

This matrix is part of a development in late medieval political theory which presented the ruler's authority as derived from the community, the ruler as servant of the community, and the end of monarchy the well-being of human individuals, rather than of corporations or grand platonic abstractions.[22] Chaucer's text supports a vision of limited monarchy, a secular power which is avowedly secular and should be exercised within limits determined by the divided community of individuals for whose interests the ruler exists. It is a vision quite in accord with the poetry's characteristic subversion of cognitive totalitarianism and dogmatic authority. It also accords with the writing's strikingly individualistic version of society. And here we meet one of the horizons of Chaucer's social imagination, for (in contrast to Langland's *Piers Plowman*) it tends to abandon all ideas of fraternity, social justice and the social embodiment of charity, foreshadowing an ideological position that would become commonplace with the triumph of bourgeois individualism in the later seventeenth and eighteenth centuries.[23]

3

Chaucer's Representations of Religion

On many occasions in *The Canterbury Tales* the officers and practices of the Church are made topics for reflection. This chapter focuses on some of the implications Chaucer's poetry held for the most powerful institution and authority in medieval Europe. Inevitably, attention can only be given to a few texts, beginning with the *Summoner's Tale*, a comic fabliau whose critical scope is characteristic of Chaucer's 'satire'.

Chaucer's *Summoner's Tale* opens with a description of a friar in Yorkshire carrying out activities that were basic to this major order of the Church—preaching and begging (ll.1709–12). He combines these activities in the local church:

> And specially, aboven every thyng,
> Excited he the peple in his prechyng
> To trentals, and to yeve, for Goddes sake,
> Wherewith men myghte hooly houses make,
> There as divine servyce is honoured,
> Nat ther as it is wasted and devoured,
> Ne ther it nedeth nat for to be yive,

As to possessioners, that mowen lyve,
Thanked be God, in wele and habundaunce.
(ll.1715-23)

Just as the *Friar's Tale* and the *Summoner's Prologue* had
worked over deep divisions in the Church, the self-styled
body of Christ, so this passage exhibits the preacher
competing with 'possessioners' for the funds of the faithful,
using the arts of rhetoric to 'excite' them to sustain his own
order. In further support of his begging and preaching, he
deploys the official teaching on purgatorial tortures and the
Church's powers to mitigate these (ll.1724-32). The passage
concludes with the wry comment:

Whan folk in chirche had yeve him what hem leste,
He wente his wey, no lenger wolde he reste.
(ll.1735-6)

The writing cultivates forms of perception which resist the
habitual separation of 'spiritual' and 'material', 'soul' and
'body', just as they resist the elevated claims of official
religious authority to transcend base material self-interest in
its own discourses and rituals. The poetry returns given
authority to the *processes* through which it is *constructed* and
imposed, processes which are rhetorical, social and economic.
Such restoration works to desublimate the kind of 'mystery'
fostered by dominant human groups who justify their
privileged status as irreplacable guardians and mediators of
this 'mystery'. Chaucer's text does not deny that the friar
preached orthodox doctrine, or deny that he sponsored
moral reform in his audience. Nor does it assert that his
practice discredits the claims of the established Church that
there is no salvation outside its own institutional apparatus
and that its clergy alone mediate grace and true doctrine. On
these matters the text remains elusively silent. It does,

however, draw attention to the economic basis of the perfectly orthodox penitential and purgatorial doctrine the cleric propagates (ll.1715–23). With this it shows how religion is a commodity and how friars must compete with other accredited salesmen (ll.1717–28). In the lines following the quoted passage, the poet depicts the friar's pastoral work after his sermon in similar terms (ll.1735–56), terms set up in the *General Prologue* (ll.208–69).

In the house of one of his supporters the friar comments on his own performance:

> I have to day been at youre chirche at messe,
> And seyd a sermon after my symple wit,
> Nat al after the text of hooly writ;
> For it is hard to yow, as I suppose,
> And therfore wol I teche yow al the glose.
> Glosynge is a glorious thyng, certeyn,
> For lettre sleeth, so as we clerkes seyn.
> There have I taught hem to be charitable,
> And spende hir good ther it is resonable;
> (ll.1788–96)

These lines present a central clerical practice, in which friars shone but all clerics took part. The activity in question is glossing, glozing or Biblical exegesis with allegory at its core. The phrase used here to justify 'glosynge', 'the letter kills', comes from a passage in St Paul (2 Corinthians 3:6) long since wrenched from its contexts and turned into a slogan to legitimise the allegorical practices of medieval exegetes and their followers. The slogan equated allegorical readings approved by orthodox clerics with the divine Spirit, while it aligned concentration on the literal sense of Biblical stories with the letter which kills, with the allegedly hard-hearted and damned Jews who refused to allegorise their sacred scriptures to fit Christian dogma. The poet sets the crucial issue of interpretation within a context where the power and self-interest of the clerical corporation is foregrounded as a basic determinant. The passage inserts the daily practice of 'glosynge' sacred texts in an institutional setting where we ourselves should remember to locate it. The 'glosynge' cleric observes that he has 'been at youre chirche at mess,/And seyd a sermon'. It is here, in church, from the authoritative height of the pulpit, with all the inevitable self-interest the text evokes, that the cleric has cast aside the literal sense of scripture, preferring the 'spiritual' gloss in approved fashion—'For lettre sleeth, so as we clerkes seyn.' Again, the poet makes explicit the material dimensions and consequences of an official spiritual practice. He discloses that the version of charity taught from the clerical pulpit, with the clerical apparatus of 'glosynge', serves the material self-interest of clerical glozers and the corporation which employs them:

> There [in church] have I taught hem [the lay audience]
>   to be charitable,
> And spend hir good ther it is resonable;

This is similar to the poet's representation of a brilliant preacher elsewhere in the *Canterbury Tales*:

> Of avarice and of swich cursednesse
> Is al my prechyng, for to make hem free
> To yeven hir pens, and namely unto me.
>   (*Pardoner's Prologue*, ll.400-2)

Chaucer's art constantly engaged with the way seemingly impersonal discourses of high authority are actually statements uttered by thoroughly embodied, partial and self-interested males, appropriating for themselves a laughably specious universality. (This fascination, and the literary mode in which it is elaborated, goes across works with formally different fictive narrators: here there is no plausible case for maintaining that the tale's poetic idiom and critical intelligence is a naturalistic projection carefully designed for the simple-minded, semi-literate 'harlot' of the *General Prologue*.)

As the poem develops, it continues the explorations I have described, concentrating on the material foundations of orthodox Christian spirituality. The friar turns the Bible to the interests of his order, claiming that when Jesus blessed the poor in spirit (Matthew 5:3) he was referring to the friars— 'in a maner glose' (ll.1919–23). The whole doctrine of evangelical poverty in the pursuit of Jesus's own pattern of life and holiness is shown as a powerful *selling* point in persuading people to support and enrich the friars rather than the secular clergy or other religious orders. The order 'wedded to poverte' ironically but significantly turns that formal marriage into grounds for the demand, 'Yif me thanne of thy gold' (ll.1907, 2099). Chaucer's text also plays with the fact that the friars' commitment to evangelical poverty had become a fiction. They had abundant corporate property, fixed incomes and a sophisticated institutional apparatus which enabled them to act effectively in secular affairs. We should not forget that the growth of their orders had been bound up with the growth of towns and the urban economy. Indeed, as Lester Little has shown, the content and the form of the friars' teaching 'was both determined by, and a determining factor within, the new urban society' with its profit-oriented economy.[1] The normality of this state of affairs by Chaucer's time is acknowledged in the depiction of the poem's friar. He is not presented as an alien monster but rather contextualised to figure how the whole apparatus of confession, penance, preaching and Biblical commentary ('glosynge') is absorbed into a culture where the cash nexus is the chief bond between people. The friar's programme is no different from the Summoner's or the Pardoner's or the

Monk's in the *General Prologue* and in the relevant tales themselves. Chaucer's writing represents the Church and its holy officials as incorrigibly immersed in a world where 'al is for to selle' (*Wife of Bath's Prologue*, l.410).

The *Summoner's Tale* finally deals with the Church's official, the priestly friar, in a manner which is both funny and coherently symbolic. The lay man, Thomas, who has given plentifully to the friars decides that they are a bad investment:

> As help me Crist, as I in fewe yeres,
> Have spent upon diverse manere freres
> Ful many a pound; yet fare I never the bet.
> Certeyn, my good have I almoost biset.
> Farwel, my gold, for it is al go!
>
> (ll.1949–53)

Clearly enough, confessor and layman share the same criteria. The priest, however, blames Thomas for spreading his investments too widely. He should have concentrated them on one order and on this one friar, 'a parfit leche' (l.1956):

> What is a ferthyng worth parted in twelve?
> Lo, ech thyng that is oned in himselve
> Is moore strong that what it is toscatered.
>
> (ll.1967–9)

Once more the friar exhibits the materialisation of spirituality fostered within the ecclesiastical framework of late medieval Europe. He calls on Thomas to help the friars 'to buylden Cristes owene chirche' (ll.1977), which again turns out, realistically enough, to be a very material structure requiring substantial economic investment, for despite donations, 'unnethe the fundement/Parfourned is' (ll.2103–4). Thomas is now enraged at the merchant of grace but the friar perseveres, attempting to convert Thomas with a long series of *exempla* against wrath (ll.1981–2093). In this, the text shows yet again how prompting a moral conversion benefits the financial aims of the official Church and its power. But the Christian layman is only apparently converted. He offers the friar a gift he must share with his brethren, and when the priest agrees,

> 'Now thanne, put in thyn hand doun by my bak,'
> Seyde this man, 'and grope wel bihynde.
> Bynethe my buttok there shaltow fynde
> A thyng that I have hyd in pryvetee.'
>
> (ll.2140–3)

Chaucer's choice of the word 'grope' links the passage with an earlier one where the friar-priest had accused parish curates of being 'ful necligent and slowe/To grope tendrely a conscience/In shrift' (ll.1816–18). Now that the metaphoric use of 'grope' is literalised, we see the remark about clerical abilities to 'grope' consciences in a fresh light, maintaining the literal meaning as we re-read the earlier passage. To make the act of examining a 'conscience' as physical as groping a 'buttok' may seem frivolous irreverence; but it is part of a chain of thought which the poet pursues throughout the bum-centred comedy of the tale's ending. The pun of 'ferthyng'/farting, when the friar begs Thomas (Thom-arse) to concentrate his investment (l.1967), and the pun on 'fundement', when he complains that 'the fundement' of their church is not yet completed and needs the aid of men like Thomas committed 'to buylden Cristes owene chirche' (ll.2103–5, 1977), both work into this chain of thought. So does Thomas's gift and the language its terms elicit. As the confessor gropes beneath the Christian's buttock,

> whan this sike man felte this frere
> Aboute his tuwel [anus] grope there and heere,

Amydde his hand he leet the frere a fart,
Ther nys no capul, drawynge in a cart,
That myghte have lete a fart of swich a soun.

(ll.2147-51)

The literalising of 'grope', the consequent reductive
embodiment of conscience, the puns already mentioned and
the crowning gift to the confessor all encourage us to
reconnect the 'spiritual' discourse of Christian 'authority'
with the material foundations ('the fundement') which such
discourse so habitually obscures and sublimates. Groping a
conscience—groping a buttock for money. 'Cristes owene
chirche' has a very material 'fundement' and this foundation,
as the text suggests, actually determines its 'spiritual' offices
and practices. The poetic comedy again invites us to
acknowledge the unity of 'spiritual' and 'material', to confess
the utterly embodied nature of human spirituality and
religious practices. In doing so it stimulates reflection about
the grounds of authority, about the material foundations of
religious activity and its official discourses.

Finally, and appropriately, the poem brings the official's
preaching from the orthodox pulpit, with which it began,
into the 'discourse' of farting. The solution to the problem of
dividing the gift among the friars includes a prominent share
for the worthy confessor. He, the squire advises, 'Shal have
the firste fruyt'. Because this befits his ecclesiastical status, so
inextricably fused with social status in the medieval Church
(ll.2260-80); and because of his preaching:

He hath to-day taught us so muche good
With prechyng in the pulpit ther he stood,
That I may vouche sauf, I sey for me.
He had the firste smel of fartes thre;

(ll.2281-4)

A fit reward for the Church's licensed preacher, wind from

one orifice rewarded by wind from another. As the lord of the village observes about Thomas:

> What, lo, my cherl, lo, yet how shrewedly
> Unto my confessour to-day he spak!
> (ll.2238-9)

The official confessor's groping and preaching bring forth an appropriate reply, speech and farting in this culture of discourse becoming indistinguishable, both determined by a material 'fundement'. (Compare here *House of Fame*, ll.765-86). The friar complains bitterly at his treatment:

> an odious meschief
> This day bityd is to myn ordre and me,
> And so, *per consequens*, to ech degree
> Of hooly chirche. . .
> (ll.2190-3)

This complaint is justified. The Church claimed to be Christ's body and the friars were an integral, officially sanctioned and privileged part of it. What many scholarly teachers and readers of Chaucer tend to overlook is that the 'odious meschief' which subverts the self-images and authority of 'hooly chirche' is Chaucer's art itself. It is not altogether surprising that many later sixteenth-century and seventeenth-century Protestants saw Chaucer, like Langland, as a rather congenial forerunner of their own attitudes to the Catholic Church, nor that many of his texts could be quite easily mobilised into their own religious discourse. Catholicity in Chaucer's day was not the Catholicity of the Counter-Reformation.

* * *

Chaucer's *Pardoner's Prologue and Tale* is one of his most

subtle and powerful performances, whose deep critical scope makes for a far more disturbing poem than the *Summoner's Tale*. A key fact to remember in reading this work is that pardoners were important official agents of the Church in the later Middle Ages. They were an established part of an increasingly elaborate system of official indulgences. Designed to offer orthodox Christians relief from punishment after death, they could easily be bought for money from accredited officials of the Church. Chaucer composed his Pardoner, as he did his Monk and Friar, as a figure who dramatises fundamental problems about contemporary religious life, the status of official authority, the nature of the Church and its claims to keep the only path to individual salvation. The pardoner's office, like the summoner's or the friar's, exemplified the absorption of the Church in the economic fabric and values of society, together with the effect this had on its 'spirituality'. Except for the open sale of confessedly false relics, the practices and theological assumptions of Chaucer's Pardoner are 'typical'.[2]

As with the Friar in the *Summoner's Tale*, Chaucer presents the Pardoner preaching 'in chirches' (1.329), emphasises his officially accredited status and then goes on to disclose the unacknowledged material foundations of the culture's most authoritative discourse and religious practices (ll.329 ff.). With penetrating irony the poet shows official preaching against cupidity, backed up by the full apparatus of spiritual authority, being used to strengthen the economic power of the Church and its officers. For people to be freed from sin is to be 'free/To yeven hir pens' to the officers of the Church (ll.400–2). So Chaucer gives the Pardoner a haunting story demonstrating the dehumanising and ruthless destructiveness of a life devoted to the accumulation of material wealth. It is a splendid 'prechyng' against 'avarice' and 'swich cursednesse' (ll.400–1). But the poet has the preacher acknowledge that he offers a 'moral tale...for to wynne', to win money (ll.460–1).

We are not encouraged to stop at analysis of the tale's form, structure or sources, to celebrate the brilliance of its formal art, or even to discuss its moral import 'in itself'. Chaucer reinserts the sermon/poem in the institutional context from which he commenced the *Pardoner's Prologue* and within which it is generated, delivered and received. It is characteristic of Chaucer's art to invite reflection on the contexts within which holy writing or speaking is made and received, to explore its role as a discursive and economic *practice* within a web of social relationships. It is seen as 'rhetoric', an art of discourse designed to persuade, to effect the practices of listeners and readers within specific conditions of production and performance.

After his sermon, the Pardoner carries on with his official and correctly licensed vocation. In a passage whose satirical depth is remarkable, Chaucer has him summon the carnival pilgrims to show their Christian devotion, to come forward, receive the Church's saving absolution and official pardon, and so secure their passage into the next world (ll.920-40). At the same time the economic drives of the Church and its dogmas concerning its own absolute necessity for human salvation are displayed—joined inseparably:

> Or elles taketh pardoun as ye wende,
> Al newe and fressh at every miles ende,
> So that ye offren, alwey newe and newe,
> Nobles or pens, whiche that be goode and trewe.
> (ll.927-30)

The gifts of grace, the acts of Christ and the movements of individuals' regeneration are transformed into aspects of a market economy in whose transactions the Church is absorbed. We are also shown a Church that has a very material interest in perpetuating endless cycles of guilt and mechanical absolution of guilt—'sin' is endless, so take, or

47

rather buy, a pardon 'newe and fressh at every miles ende'. The fear of death is profitably cashed by the institution which claimed to control the 'treasury' of merit created by Christ's sacrifice:

> Paraventure ther may fallen oon or two
> Doun of his hors, and breke his nekke atwo.
> Looke which a seuretee is it to yow alle
> That I am in youre felaweshipe yfalle,
> That may assoille yow, bothe moore and lasse,
> Whan that the soule shal fro the body passe.
> (ll.935–40)

The Institution and its officials create the fear of other-worldly tortures and propagate doctrines which make the faithful dependent on them for 'seuretee' in their working earthly pilgrimage from the pub to church to pub.

Chaucer's text does not only work over the practices, language and ideology of the Church. It represents the collusion of the Christian laity: its habitual deference to authority (a deference which may also be a comfortably secure evasion of critical reflection), its participation in the marketing of religion, and its fusion of magic with religion. Without this collusion the Pardoner would not be possible.[3] In many ways, figures like the Pardoner thus also symbolise important features of popular religiosity. Certainly, the Pardoner and his clients, the holy corporation employing him and the Christian laity sustaining that Church, are bound together in a unity which by Chaucer's time was not without severe tensions and contradictions. (The European Reformation had an enabling pre-history.)

The text itself refracts such tensions and is produced within them. Its implications for the orthodox could be rather grim. For the poem negated the reliability of the institution on which Christians were supposed to depend for their eternal salvation. It undermined the Church's claims to impersonal, disinterested, transcendent authority; mocked, and undermined, its claims to dispense saving pardons and absolutions; mocked its claims about holy relics and their powers ('pigges bones', *General Prologue*, l.700; *Pardoner's Prologue*, l.347-9); and subverted its elevated discourses, its 'predicacioun' splattered with the language of the clerical élite designed to overawe the laity (ll.329-46). More disturbingly still, the text does not leave the laity any criteria for distinguishing the 'true' from the 'false' pardoner/ relic/absolution/'predicacioun', a task which the Catholic Church insisted was not the laity's anyway. Trust the office and ignore the deviations of the officers, was the official line. But this text discredits such comforting distinctions. If the institution ordinary people supported with their tithes, gifts, payments and obedience was felt to be in the state represented by the text, where could they turn for reliable guarantees that their daily lives could be squared with God's demands and their salvation secured? Unexamined conventional piety, faith in the established Church, the 'seuretee' its officers bring, this could well be the practice of an unChristian life whose beneficiary in the present life was a very worldly corporation staffed by thoroughly fleshly officers; and in the future life, the only beneficiary might be Satan. This was the position reached by many medieval heretics, including the English Lollards.[4] But while Chaucer had good friends who were Lollards, he himself does not instruct anyone. He is, self-consciously, no authority. His text leaves its readers to cope with its vision of the Church as seems appropriate to them. He does, however, represent one possible, perhaps very likely, response to his disturbing text and holds that up for critical scrutiny. He gives this response to the Host and it is apparently unchallenged by the other good Christian people on this pilgrimage, itself a potent image of the secularisation of a 'spiritual' practice.

The Host is consistently presented as a conventional bourgeois Christian, hostile to any hints of nonconformism, proudly exhibiting the stereotyped marks of male egoism and aggression, piously sentimental (*General Prologue*, l.754; *Man of Law's Tale*, ll.1173-7; *Parson's Tale*, l.38; *Prologue to Monk's Tale*, ll.1943-62; *Merchant's Tale*, ll.2419-40). Untroubled by any touch of his maker's critical imagination, he enjoys the unexamined life with gusto. His reaction to the Pardoner's troubling disclosure is appropriate to the commonplace figure Chaucer composed. He bursts out in a self-righteous and personal attack on the Pardoner:

> I wolde I hadde thy coillons [balls] in myn hond
> In stide of relikes or of seintuarie.
> Lat kutte hem of, I wol thee helpe hem carie;
> They shul be shryned in an hogges toord!
>
> (ll.952-5)

This violence allows that Host to ignore the profoundly disturbing issues raised through Chaucer's poem and his Pardoner. It turns the individual Pardoner into a scapegoat for the massive problems and anxieties in the late medieval Church, ones that were to prove intractable. The Host assumes that by crushing (and castrating) the Pardoner the problems dramatised through his performance will simply disappear. This kind of response is still found in readings which fail to grasp the representative nature of the Pardoner and the manner in which the poem explores decisive contradictions and crisis in the official Church. Chaucer aligns such a limited response with the mentality figured forth in his Host. Instead of facing distressing institutional, intellectual and religious difficulties for what they are, individual scapegoats are singled out, substituted for the real problems and then destroyed. Any threat to the 'seuretee' of conventional piety must be suppressed; any voice that stimulates uncomfortable and potentially subversive reflection must be silenced; the abyss must be decently veiled with simple-minded pieties and certainties, however anomalous and remote from contemporary practices these have become. When the other pilgrims see the Pardoner attacked and silenced, they laugh (ll.956–7, 961). True, the Knight asks Host and Pardoner to kiss: he too wishes to veil the abyss, preserving the precarious cohesion of the group, substituting laughter (not necessarily simple) for the meditation Chaucer's text stimulates and embodies (ll.960–7). Some readers will choose to respond with the Host or the Knight; or in some variation on that response. But others will refuse that reaction. For these, Chaucer's writing continues to undermine the uncritical acceptance of authority and its self-images, the conventional separation of the 'spiritual' or 'ideal' from the social, economic and material dimensions of human being. For these readers this text is a supreme and characteristic moment in Chaucer's poetry, revealing his critical power as he works over major problems of authority in the religious practices and discourses of his culture.

* * *

The *Canterbury Tales* includes a few poems which take the general form of saints' legends. The genre they represent exhibits some of the most mechanistic and materialistic supernaturalism in late medieval Christianity. Nothing could be more alien to the productions of this genre than the critical imagination and literary modes we meet in most of Chaucer's writings. Why then did Chaucer use this genre at all? Some argue that he did so to suspend his critical irony, as he did in his *Retractions*, to celebrate a conventional form of sentimental piety. This is not an implausible position. No writer's work is necessarily coherent or free from internal contradictions: he or she will confront a range of different pressures at different stages in life and will evolve different responses in changing circumstances. Nevertheless, my own view is that the *Canterbury Tales*, made in a heterogeneous religious culture, included some writing in this genre to test it out, to explore it, to bring out the central features and mentality it encapsulated, to encourage critical detachment from its methods and the ideology it carried. I shall try to illustrate this contention, however briefly, because these legends represent certain basic attitudes in militant Christianity and because Chaucer's versions are now often taken as examples of his unironic participation in the commonplaces of late medieval piety.

In the *Second Nun's Tale*, Saint Cecilie is an upper-class lady whose sole vocation is 'to kepe hir maydenhede' (ll. 120–6). She does not refuse to be married but at the wedding feast secretly asks God to keep her un-spotted (ll.127–40). It is typical of the degradation of specifically sexual love in Christian culture that this holy person should assume marital sexual love inevitably involves sin (see Chapter 4). She tells her husband that if he touches her an angel will slaughter him, classifying marital sex as 'love in vileynye' (ll.151–8). This is characteristic of a familiar enough form of militant Christianity: self-righteous, violent, prepared to kill in the name of 'love'. Such Christian chastity was offered a lesson by Chaucer's contemporary Langland:

> Chastite wiþouten charite worþ [will be] cheyned in helle;
> It is as lewed as a lampe þat no liȝt is Inne
> *(Piers Plowman, B, I.188–9)*

Chaucer's own poetry both provides contexts for problematising the model good life such saints' legends projected, and shows the grave limitations of this popular literary genre as a medium for any intelligent moral or psychological reflection.

The *Second Nun's Tale* offers further examples of the piety fostered by the orthodox mentality that produced saints' legends. Christian 'faith' becomes a matter of allegedly unambiguous *empirical* verification. Visible angels appear bearing sweet-smelling roses and lilies (typically literalised symbols); the converted Christian sees the angel of God 'every day', 'in tyme and space'; and, better still, 'every maner boone/That he God axed, it was sped ful soone' (ll.355-7). The next two lines comment mockingly on this magical, materialistic Christianity and the saints' legends that propagated it:

> It were ful hard by ordre for to seyn
> How manye wondres Jhesus for hem wroghte;
> (ll.358-9)

The externalisation and mechanisation of 'grace' (l.354), so pervasive in late medieval popular religious writing and practice, is shown as part of an infantile fantasy. This bestows total power over a benevolent magic guaranteed to gratify the Christian's insatiable ego.

The *Second Nun's Tale* also reflects how in this genre the simply good, elect Christians duly confront the simply bad non-Christians to receive the treatment the Church itself handed out to heretics—death. The execution of Christians is accompanied by the conventional paraphernalia of very earthly miracles which act as religious 'proofs'. One convert converts people (and bolsters up the readers' 'faith'?) by telling them he actually saw the souls of two executed brethren glide to heaven escorted by angels (ll.400-4). What status, what religious meaning could such allegedly empirical claims have? What would such sightings actually 'prove'? Chaucer's art invites us to consider such matters and the construction of such discourses, whereas saints' legends, like all homiletic writings, strive to overwhelm critical reflexivity.

In the saint's death Chaucer's text again displays basic features of the genre in a satiric context. The governor orders that Cecile be burnt in a fire-bath (as a heretic). But the Christian lady, immersed in a fire all night:

> sat al coold, and feelede no wo.
> It made hire nat a drope for to sweete.
>
> (ll.521–2)

The emphasis in recording the detail of the last line is part of a comedy directed against a literary tradition and the religious mentality that inhabited it. It culminated in the final scene where the governor's executioner tries to chop off the saint's head but cannot 'smyte al hir nekke atwo' (ll.526–8). As the law forbids a fourth stroke he leaves Cecile 'half deed, with hir nekke ycorven there', free to preach the virtues of militant Christianity to admiring audiences for three days while they mop up the blood with 'sheetes' (ll.535–9). (Chaucer does not explore the sadistic and pornographic dimensions of saints' legends.) Once again 'faith' becomes a matter of empirical events 'proving' the dogmas of Christianity and the authority of the Church. With this, the poet concludes a nice example of a widespread religious genre whose moral, imaginative and religious forms and presuppositions he has held up for our reflection.

This approach may be appropriate for reading another poem in the genre, the *Prioress's Tale*. The poem discloses how violence and brutality pervade some of the most favoured religious forms and emotions ('pity', 'pathos') in late medieval piety. We are shown how Christian sentimentality mistakes itself for, and is often mistaken for, love and compassion. The kind of piety evoked and satirised in this text is carried by a cult of supposedly child-like innocence—'litel sone', 'litel child', 'litel book', 'litel scole', 'smale children', 'sely child', the diminutives are repeated, cloyingly. In this poem it seems as though Chaucer has chosen to continue the satirisation of the Prioress in the *General Prologue* (ll.118–62), writing in a narrative voice which presents itself as having the stereotypically and quite unchild-like 'child-like' simplicity it values so highly:

> My konnyng is so wayk, o blisful Queene,
> . . .
> But as a child of twelf month oold, or lesse,
> Than kan unnethes any word expresse.
> (*Prioress's Tale*, ll.481, 484–5)

The text reveals how such piety and the far from simple literary forms through which we encounter it block out all critical self-awareness encouraging grossly destructive models of 'love'.

In the opening stanza of the tale, the poet has the Prioress introduce the local Jews as automatically 'Hateful to Crist and to his compaignye' (l.492). Typical of much in the history of Christian practice, the teller assumes for herself a full knowledge of divine judgement, revealing her assumption that racial and religious hatred is a perfectly unproblematic part of Christianity. The clash between this stance and the outlook of Jesus in the Gospels is quite lost in the tradition she figures, but hardly lost on her creator. The teller's much-discussed anti-semitism burns through the performance and is representative of the virulent racism that has pervaded Christian culture and has actually been fostered by certain versions of the religion. All this is critically placed within the text as a whole, which also evokes another perspective on Christian anti-Semitism, one that is sometimes overlooked. In the first stanza Chaucer has the Prioress relate that the Jews were

Sustened by a lord of that contree
For foule usure and lucre of vilenye
(ll.490–1)

This calls up the history of the Jews in Christian Europe: the
Jews' legal status and economic practices had been entirely
controlled by Christian rulers who had used and exploited
them. This relationship evokes another major factor in
Christian anti-Semitism. Namely, Christians could use Jews
to service aspects of their own profit economy which
traditional ethics still regarded with hostility and classified as
'usury'. Here, as Lester Little has argued, Christians could
'project their own guilt on to the Jews', inventing a whole
anti-Semitic mythology complete with stories like the one
Chaucer gives to his Prioress.[5] The poet emphasises the
representative, generic nature of the Prioress's story by
having her also recall:

O younge Hugh of Lyncoln, slayn also
With cursed Jewes, as it is notable,
For it is but a litel while ago
(ll.684–6)

This alludes to the charge of ritual murder brought against
Jews in Lincoln in 1255 after which nineteen Jews were
hanged without trial by the good Christian citizens.[6] In her
tale there is similarly no trial, and the ruler organises the
summary killing of all Jews assumed to have known about
the murder of the child (ll.628–34). The ruler, uncriticised
by the pious Prioress who weeps if a man strikes one of her
pampered dogs (*General Prologue*, ll.143–9), invokes the Old
Testament rule of an eye for an eye a tooth for a tooth, a law
explicitly superseded in Jesus's teachings on love and non-
retaliation against violence.[7] The text further sharpens the
ironic perspectives cast on such Christian love as the

Prioress's and its popular literary genres. It does so by following the ruler's praise of Christ and his mother, given her traditional accolade 'welle of mercy' (ll.617–19, 656), with the decision to drag the Jews about with wild horses before hanging them. Richard Schoeck seems right to see 'in Chaucer's treatment of the Prioress a clear-eyed recognition of the inhumanity of her Tale, its violation of the deepest sense of charity'.[8] But Chaucer's imagination has, as usual, not just explored or satirised the idiosyncratic viciousness of one deviant individual Christian. Rather, his writing has displayed a *representative* and important strand in con- temporary Christian piety and its cultures of discourse.

Some readers may, however unfashionably, want to ask whether it is possible to identify an unequivocally 'Chaucerian' religious stance that lies 'behind' the literary procedures we have been analysing. Our chief interest, of course, must be in the literary productions, the contexts within which they were produced, where they first achieved human meaning and the meanings the texts have as we inevitably recontextualise them in the present. We do not have access to the consciousness of Chaucer 'behind' the discourses we have. Nevertheless, for those who may wish to construct a model of 'Chaucer's religion' which may go beyond the boundaries of our evidence, a few brief and rather speculative suggestions are offered. Perhaps they could be pursued by others.

First it would be worth noting some *absences* in Chaucer's work considered as the production of a late medieval Christian writer encompassing a wide variety of genres and styles, absences which could be focused by a comparison with the great contemporary poem by Langland, *Piers Plowman*. A list of such absences would at least include the following: absence of attention to the incarnate Christ and theology of incarnation; absence of meditation on the relations between individual salvation and the act of the incarnate, suffering, crucified Christ; absence of any marked sense that salvation entails an imitation of Jesus's life and commitments; absence of the poor Christ or traditional cult of poverty; despite a preoccupation with free will and determinism, an absence of meditation on specifically *Christian* problems of grace, free will, God's foreknowledge and predestination; absence of any concern with the historical dimensions of Christianity and their versions of salvation; absence of any specifications for reform of the Church, in contrast to both orthodox reformers and heretical ones—although some of his own friends were upper-class Lollards; absence of any signs of the Christian mysticism which flourished in fourteenth-century Europe; absence even of that increasingly internalised, affective personal devotion and intimacy with Christ manifested in much late medieval religious writing; absence of conventional religious allegory other than as material to be worked critically. This list is by no means exhaustive.

Even the *Parson's Tale* does not affect this situation, despite many pious critics' attempts to make this the unironic code through which all Chaucer's writing must be read. The long prose work attributed to the Parson is a translation, with some adaptation, of standard works on penitence, the seven mortal sins and remedies against them. Placed in *The Canterbury Tales* it becomes part of a fiction-making competition whose reward is a free dinner in a London pub (as Lydgate's *Siege of Thebes* recalled). We approach it as one attempt, by one of the pilgrims, to give his version of 'the way' (*Parson's Prologue*, ll.22–73). Furthermore, we observe that this pilgrim is subjected to some satirical treatment. For example, in the joke against the Parson who proudly tells his audience:

> Thou getest fable noon ytoold for me;
> For Paul, that writeth unto Thymothee,

Repreveth hem that weyven soothfastnesse,
And tellen fables and swich wrecchednesse,
Why shold I sowen draf out of my fest,
Whan I may sowen whete, if that me lest?
(ll.31–6)

This simple-minded, if traditional, contempt for fiction is placed within a magnificent collection of poetic fables on which Chaucer was still working when he died. Through it the poet again glances at conventional assurance that authoritative humans have quite unproblematic and totally impersonal access to objective truth which they grasp unaffected, even unmediated by their own embodied, historically contingent and avowedly sinful being. Chaucer's work, as we have seen, explodes such illusions, encouraging far more complex ideas about human knowledge and a far more modest awareness of its limits. His poetry constantly blocks off such allegedly transcendental certainty beyond discourse and beyond the boundaries of a specific social world. We have no cause to treat the Parson's performance unquestioningly. On top of this, it seems that Chaucer altered the sources from which he was translating to compose a Parson-teller whose views on sexual matters and marriage represent a hard-line orthodoxy treated with great critical power in his own work.[9] Furthermore, the contrast between the literary mode of the *Parson's Tale* and Chaucer's writing on similar topics elsewhere helps us grasp the *limitations* of the former.[10] Here, certainly, is no 'key' to 'Chaucer'.

If I had to hypothesise some quasi-philosophical framework congenial to Chaucer's writings, I would choose an undogmatic ethical stoicism. That Chaucer translated Boethius's *Consolation of Philosophy* and often addresses or uses this work which contains nothing specifically Christian is a fact that might be hard to interpret. What could perhaps

59

be less ambiguous is the group of neo-Stoic Boethian lyrics ('The former age', 'Fortune', 'Truth', 'Gentilesse', 'Lak of Stedfastnesse'). Characteristic of these texts' stance is the following:

> Tempest thee noght al croked to redresse,
> In trust of hir that turneth as a bal:
> Gret rest stant in litel besinesse;
> Be war also to sporne ayeyns an al;
> Stryve not, as doth the crokke with the wal.
> Daunte thyself, that dauntest otheres dede;
> And trouthe thee shal delivere, it is no drede.
>
> ('Truth', ll.8–14)

Such writing exhibits an individualism quite free from any orthodox Christian sense of original sin, unconcern with divine grace mediated through the acts of Christ and the Catholic Church or the need for prevenient grace if anything is to be done 'wel' (1.6) and acceptably to God. The poem as a whole assumes that the individual unaided by divine grace is capable of virtuous self-organisation (ll.1–7), a position anathematised as 'pelagian' in traditional Christian doctrine. The individual's virtuous activity is utterly independent from the instruction, control and penitential apparatus of the official Church. Typically this is not asserted in an 'heretical' or 'dissident' mode: the Catholic Church is simply absent—just as it is in the final work of Chaucer's Lollard friend, Clanvowe (*The two ways*).

The stanza quoted from 'Truth', also reveals an outlook that may well be part of the reflexivity informing so much of Chaucer's writing. The counsel is that no struggle to change, to *reform* the 'croked' ways of the historical world should be taken on. Such struggle is allegedly doomed for the dominant 'croked' ways are unreformable and will only destroy the reformer—advice elaborated in the third stanza.

This stoic stance is as far removed from the drives of orthodox Christian reformers of the later Middle Ages as from unorthodox ones. As I have remarked, it is singularly independent of even the Gospels, let alone of official Christian institutions and dogmatics. The vision is pessimistic: the social world is unreformable, the 'croked' are best left alone, no human being can do anything to help others or improve anything. But, perhaps typical of most versions of Stoicism, it is also profoundly conformist. The individual's critical detachment, his own critical reflexivity, is part of a detachment which allows the Stoic to combine the sharpest critical perspective with ironical, indeed self-ironising, accommodation to the status quo. This accommodation allows the full appropriation of the fruits of conformism and avoids all the risks and penalties of nonconformism. Furthermore, such a stance exhibits an individualism which remains sceptical of all ideals of 'community'—itself a product and a nourisher of social fragmentation. It is not surprising, in this perspective, that Chaucer's writing should be replete with self-images of the poet's *isolation*, his aloneness, combined with the representations of a social collective marked by the individualism, incohesion and fragmentation examined in Chapter 2. Perhaps Chaucer's critical imagination, his witty yet profound engagement with the forms of authority and the limits of human knowing, his penetrating exploration of the contradictions and problems in official Christianity as he perceived it, all these could have nourished something like the accommodating stoical individualism I have just constructed. This might merge with the proto-bourgeois individualism suggested at the close of my previous chapter. And, perhaps, it may be one small contributing factor to his canonisation by academics who construct 'English Literature' with its apparatus of set texts and examinations.

4

Chaucer's Representations of Marriage and Sexual Relations

Over thirty years ago an American scholar studying medieval romances wrote:

> It is a commonplace that throughout the Middle Ages marriage was an arrangement of convenience, an enforced legal contract designed to secure certain political, military, or economic advantages. With such ends in view, it was inevitable that the desire of the woman should be the least significant element in the bargain.[1]

Although the evidence supporting Margaret Gist's statement is overwhelming, the 'commonplace' she outlines with the link she rightly makes between the material foundations of marriage and the dismissal of female desire in a patriarchal society, is still not often foregrounded by teachers of medieval literature. Her summary of the basis of Christian marriage points us towards the contexts in which human beings experienced marriage and its sexuality. These were the contexts within which, and potentially against which, imaginative explorations of marriage took place.

The mentality fostered by respectable medieval marriages can be illustrated from the diary for a fourteenth-century merchant, Georgio Dati:

> I had an illegitimate male child by Margherita, a Tartar slave whom I had bought... [1391] We [business associates] renewed our partnership on 1 January 1393, when I undertook to invest 1,000 [gold] florins. I did not actually have the money but was about to get married—which I then did—and to receive the dowry which procured me a larger share and more consideration in our company...I married my second wife, Betta, on 22 June. ...On the 26th of that same June, I received a payment of 800 gold florins from the bank of Giacomino and Co. This was the dowry...On 5 July 1402...Betta gave birth to our eighth child. After that my wife Betta passed to Paradise. ... The [business] partnership is to start on 1 January 1403 and to last three years...I have undertaken to put up 2,000 florins. This is how I propose to raise them; 1,370 florins are still due to me from my old partnership... . The rest I expect to obtain if I marry again this year, when I hope to find a woman with a dowry as large as God may be pleased to grant me.

'God' duly obliged the merchant, and he records that in May 1403 he was betrothed and 'The dowry was 1,000 florins: 700 in cash and 300 in a farm'. He had eleven children by this wife. She died in childbirth, 'after lengthy suffering', and he writes: 'I then took another wife. . . . The dowry was 600 florins...'.[2] This man is in no way deviant. His diary exemplifies what Gist correctly described as 'commonplace'; a respectable man's outlook and the practice of Christian marriage in a society like the Wife of Bath's where 'al is for to selle' (*Wife of Bath's Prologue*, l.414). The human effects of this economic foundation to medieval Christian marriage can hardly be ignored.

Another major force shaping the contexts in which

Chaucer lived and out of which he wrote is orthodox Christian teaching on marriage and marital sex, the norms the Church *tried* to impose from the pulpit, through the apparatus of the confessional, through a massive array of didactic writings, through formal theological and legal texts. Chaucer's fictions work over the conventional teachings I shall summarise, put them into solution, explore them and their likely effects on human identity and relationship. Grasping the ideological contexts of his poetry here will help us engage with the resonances of the texts we study and help us grasp the achievements and horizons of his imagination.

The chief purposes of Christian marriage were the procreation of children to be reared in the orthodox Catholic Church, and the channelling of sexual drives: without such marriage, by definition, 'fornication' would flourish. The Church proved incapable of seeing that the deepest love could be fully and profoundly expressed in sexual union. Indeed, it constantly excluded the expression of mutual love and delight as a legitimate purpose of specifically sexual union between married people. The prevalent clerical attitude was authoritatively expressed by St Augustine: 'I feel that nothing more turns the masculine mind from the heights than female blandishments and the contact of bodies without which a wife may not be had' (*Soliloquies*, I.10). No wonder the Church prohibited priests from marriage. Nor is it surprising that this outlook should become articulated in an ideology which taught that focus on the enjoyment of sexual union within marriage was a sin, probably a mortal sin. It is characteristic of this tradition that Pope Gregory the Great forbade people to enter a church or receive communion after marital sex because he feared that all sex involved some pleasure of the flesh which entailed sin. J. T. Noonan's comment is relevant: 'A barrier was set against the consideration of marital values other than procreation; consideration of a value such as love was blocked.'[3] Similarly,

H. A. Kelly found that in doctrines about the purposes of Christian marriage taught by theologians and canonists (church lawyers), 'mutual love between the spouses is notably absent'.[4] In fact, as Noonan's research shows, throughout the Middle Ages 'there is no integration of the ideal of personal love with the purpose of [marital] intercourse.'[5] This Christian tradition had powerful propagandists and its mark on our culture was to be long-lasting. William Blake was still struggling with its survival in the nineteenth century, as he writes in his magnificent *Jerusalem*:

> Have you known the Judgement that is arisen among the
> Zoas of Albion? where a Man dare hardly to embrace
> His own Wife, for the Terrors of Chastity that they call
> By the name of Morality.

On the contrary,

> every Minute Particular is Holy:
> Embraces are Comminglings: from the Head even to the Feet
> (*Jerusalem*, Plates 32 and 69)

But instead of Blake, let us listen to some orthodox Christian voices, remembering that these passages are explicitly about sexual love between couples married within the Christian sacrament of marriage.

We catch the core of the tradition in the infinitely repeated formula asserting that 'the too ardent lover of his own wife is an adulterer'. Instructing confessors on how to be guided in their inquiries into the lives of married people, J.P. Foresti advised:

> If one was too immodest in touches, embraces, kisses and other dishonourable things [*inhonesta*], it sometimes might be mortally sinful because these things are not consonant with sacred

matrimony. ... If he knew [sexually] his wife not for offspring
or for paying the debt [i.e. the so-called marital debt to alleviate
the spouse's lust, to prevent adultery], but only for his own
insatiable and uncontrollable pleasure ... he has exposed himself
to the danger of serious sin.[6]

It was only a licit intercourse, 'paying of the debt' (the
adoption of such Pauline language itself tells a revealing
story), if the spouse did so *without* intention of taking any
pleasure in the sexual act. This is standard teaching which
Chaucer knew in detail.

He translated its stock commonplaces in the penitential
manual he gives to the Parson as his 'myrie tale in prose' in
those unfinished writings he called 'the tales of Caunterbury'
(*Retractions*). As noted in the last chapter, there are grounds
for reading the *Parson's Tale* and its *Prologue* as involving a
critical treatment of both Parson and the orthodox Christian
line on marital sex.[7] Whatever readers may finally decide
about the place of this work, it at least demonstrates
Chaucer's intimate knowledge of fully-elaborated Christian
ideology in the sphere of marital sex. His writing discloses
that his fascination was with the human implications of
standard Christian teaching, and its explorations were
profoundly imaginative and highly critical.

Let us stay with the *Parson's Tale* for a moment. Having
used the word 'ordure' to denote excrement (1.428), the
Parson proclaims that married couples who make love in and
for mutual 'delit' commit the mortal sin of adultery, proving
the devil himself has control over them and that they have
'yven hemself to alle ordure' (ll.903–5). With relish he
proclaims the Christian view of the eternal punishment
'adulterers' will suffer 'in helle in a stank brennynge of fyr
and of brymston' (1.840). The only kind of marital sex the
Parson approves is a joyless penitential suffering: 'she hath
merite of chastitee that yeldeth to her housbonde the dette of

hir body, ye, though it be agayn hir likynge and the lust of hire herte' (1.940). The human consequences of such ideas of virtue can be painfully followed in Margery Kempe's account of her own marital experiences, an account that should be read and carefully considered by all interested in medieval writing and culture as well as by those studying specifically female experiences in our history.[8] (Comparison between her work and Chaucer's could also focus on Chaucer's horizons and the limits of his insight.) Chaucer himself depicted some aspects of the appalling human reality such Christian ideology fostered in his representation of May and the Wife of Bath enduring their Christian husbands' unwanted sexual intercourse, practising what the Parson describes as the 'merite...that yeldeth to hire housbonde the dette of hir body...agayn hir likynge'. The Parson's text drives home conventional Christian ideology: 'if they [a married couple] assemble oonly for amorous love...to accomplice thilke brennynge delit...it is deedly synne' (1.942). The teaching and its language manifest the complete degradation of the erotic, the total separation of love from sexuality, of sexuality from one's full and true humanity. It is just here that the Christian ideology of sex joins hands with the most degenerate pornography to fragment the human person, to split off and debase sexual love. The Parson's ideal is a sexless marriage: 'Man sholden loven hys wyf...as thogh it were his suster' (1.860). (He is not, presumably, recommending incest!)

There is one more point worth making about the Christian doctrine displayed in the *Parson's Tale*. That is, its unexamined but characteristic union with the economic foundations and interests of marriage, ones under exclusively male control. For example, in treating adultery the text describes this as including sin against *property* rights: 'This synne is eek a thefte; for thefte generally is for to reve a wight his thyng' (1.876). The woman is represented as a mere

67

object, a piece of property owned by the Christian male, 'his thyng'. Furthermore, through adulteries, 'comen false heires ofte tyme, that wrongfully occupien folkes heritages. And therefore [sic!] wol Crist putte hem out of the regne of hevene, that is heritage to goode folk' (l.883). Whereas Christ in the New Testament taught and followed a path of poverty, of disengagement from property, family and wealth, orthodox Christianity managed to turn him into the great defender of established property rights, punishing humans with eternal torments for breaking the patterns of family inheritance of property.

This combination of economic structure and interests joined with Christian sexual ideology to shape medieval marriages. It is the material that formed the dominant contexts and horizons with which Chaucer's fictions work, actively, in powerful imaginative exploration. Whether the specifically literary heritage of romance and courtly poems of love offered important and genuinely alternative models of sexual relations is a question I shall take up later in this chapter.

* * *

In discussing Chaucer's representations of society we considered the significance of the *Shipman's Tale* and I now wish to recall that poem. Chaucer left signs that he attributed it at some stage to a female speaker, presumably the Wife of Bath (ll.10–19). It displays very crisply the fate of marital and extramarital sexual relations in the world it figures. If the practice and ethos of the market pervades a society, if human relations become predominantly mediated through a cash nexus, the forms human sexuality takes and the language in which they are spoken, will be profoundly affected. The *Shipman's Tale* displays this in a thoroughly jovial mode. The merchant's wife views sexual activity as an economic exchange: in exchange for her husband's support she will 'paye' him in bed, simultaneously fulfilling the Church's command that spouses should 'pay the debt' (ll.413-24). She perceives her own body as a commodity. Her genitals become an account-book, and the poem concludes with a pun which fuses genitals, the sexual act, the poem itself and financial accounting:

> For I wol paye yow wel and redily
> Fro day to day, and if so be I faille,
> I am youre wyfe; score it upon my taille,
> And I shal paye as soon as ever I may.
> . . .
> Thus endeth now my tale, and God us sende
> Taillynge ynough unto our lyves ende.
> (ll.414-17, 433-4)

Nor is extramarital sex any different. The wife agrees with the monk, 'That for thise hundred frankes he sholde al nyght/Have hire in his armes bolt upright' (ll. 314-15). Crude, but symbolising the kind of crude reduction of human relations where the cash nexus is central.

Chaucer elaborates his vision of this situation in the poem he did give to the Wife of Bath. Her famous *Prologue* exhibits the fate of woman as a commodity to be bought and used in marriage, one whose economic and religious task was to 'pay the debt' in a society where 'al is for to selle' (l. 414). In exchange for the sexual use of her body, her first three husbands give her economic security (ll. 204, 212). This has been a normal enough state of affairs in our civilisation but Chaucer's satire brings out its nastiness:

> For wynnyng wolde I al his lust endure,
> And make me a feyned appetit;
> And yet in bacon hadde I nevere delit,

That made me that evere I wolde hem chide.
(ll. 416–19)

The frustration and degradation of sexual life in such a culture is sharply evoked. It is one, as we noted above, supported by the Church's command to 'pay the debt': the Wife has good cause to cry out, 'Allas! allas! that evere love was synne!' (l. 614). Yet, as in the passage just quoted, Chaucer shows how she, like the wife in the *Shipman's Tale*, accepts the practices and ethos of the market. She rebels against male domination, confirming the fears embodied in the anti-feminist tradition she knows so well and judges so accurately as the outpourings of psychically crippled and unreflexive males (ll. 692–710). But she does so within the framework of market relations, and seeks power through the accumulation of property, grounded in the sale of her labour-power and her body. As Alfred David observes, she 'regards "love" like any other commodity to be bought and sold in the world's market place'.[9] The attitudes of this female rebel thus give us further insight into a culture which teaches her that marriage is a relationship grounded in the exchange of commodities and the domination of one human by another. Even when she achieves the freedom to marry 'for love and no richesse' (l. 526) she claims to 'love' her young husband because he was stand-offish, thus making himself a more valuable commodity to the purchasing Wife:

> Greet prees at market maketh deere ware;
> And to greet cheep is holde at litel prys:
> (ll. 522–3; see too ll. 513–16)

The language discloses a form of life, the culture which generates it. That her fifth marriage fails to transcend the economic conflicts and struggles for domination fostered in her society, is hardly surprising (ll. 627–827).

* * *

In the *Merchant's Tale* Chaucer offers one of the most disturbing visions of traditional Christian marriage as an institutionalisation of human and sexual degradation. Its critical perspective, subtlety, imagistic resonance and overall organisation cannot meaningfully be attributed to the perverse shallowness of the misogynistic merchant who is its formal pilgrim-teller. As throughout the *Canterbury Tales*, there is simply no hard-and-fast rule about the relations between author, fictional tellers and tales, nor is there always a consistent narrative voice in even one tale. It is important that the reader neither seeks nor imposes the kind of 'coherence' here that Chaucer's texts seem quite uninterested in.

The poem opens with a lengthy and ironic reflection on normal male assumptions about the ends of marriage—that is, the 'paradys terrestre' the male hopes to experience in marriage, and the risks he runs of not having his expectations matched (ll. 1245–468). This passage is replete with long-lasting masculine stereotypes of women, fixing their role as the male's obedient eonomic, domestic and, of course, sexual instrument. She is also, inevitably, the lost, nurturing and all-accepting mother. The old knight who wants a wife is affluent enough to afford a wide range of choice. Chaucer presents this activity in a brilliantly evocative image:

> Heigh fantasye and curious bisynesse
> Fro day to day gan in the soule impresse
> Of Januarie about his mariage.
> Many fair shap and many a fair visage
> Ther passeth thurgh his herte nyght by nyght
> As whoso tooke a mirour, polisshed bryght,
> And sette it in a commune market-place,

71

Thanne sholde he se ful many a figure pace
By his mirour...

(ll. 1577–85)

Here again are the possible psychic consequences of inhabiting a society where, in the Wife of Bath's words, 'al is for to selle'. In this imaging, women are, typically enough, denied all subjectivity—they only exist as objects in the acquisitive male field of vision, commodities to be purchased and consumed.

This version, as already noted, has its material foundations in contemporary social organisation and Chaucer proceeds to illustrate normal practices in the arrangement of *respectable* marriages. The knight's kin and friends make the legal and economic contracts whereby the woman he desires 'Shal wedded be unto this Januarie' (ll. 1692–8). The female's desire, as Margaret Gist observed about the reality of standard marriages, is irrelevant, written out. She is made totally passive. Any genuine marriage will, of course, be an orthodox Christian one, a holy sacrament, and Januarie's is certainly that—a church wedding blessed by the priest (ll. 1700–8). Chaucer emphasises the role of the Church, for after the wedding feast he shows the passive bride being 'broght abedde as stille as stoon' and the priest blessing the bed of the marriage the Church has sanctified (ll.1818–9). Thus the text reveals the total involvement of the Church (something that was a long struggle for it to achieve) in the perpetuation of a marital institution based on economic power and male enthralment of females. As Chaucer evokes the meaning of loveless marriage and the compulsory sex that went with it, we may remember J.T. Noonan's analysis of the Church's 'failure to incorporate love into the purpose of marital intercourse'.[10] The poet's satire embraces the ideology and practices of the Catholic Church in a way that many pious commentators and teachers still evade. He makes the priest's blessing of the bed lead straight into the sharply detailed and hideous representation of aggressive sexuality, the death of tenderness and the absence of any mutuality—an outstanding passage too long to quote here (ll. 1820–50). Marital sex is exhibited as an arena where the male may use the female body in a self-gratifying exercise of 'manly' power and domination. Chaucer's finely particularised satire evokes and decisively judges male attitudes which are still manifest, be it in living reality, in pornography, or in 'respectable' literature such as Lawrence's *The Plumed Serpent* or parts of *Lady Chatterley's Lover*.[11] Male sexuality is presented, in an image often chosen by men, as a 'knyf', a weapon used 'on the job' to carve up the 'yong flessh', 'the tendre veel' in terms of which the woman has already been imagined (ll. 1840, 1832–3, 1418–20; c.f. *Parson's Tale*, ll. 855–60). Chaucer concludes this memorable passage by inviting his readers to reflect on a perspective habitually occluded both in traditional literature and its conventional teaching in our institutions of education: 'God woot what that May thoughte in hir herte' (l.1851). Or, as he ironically asks us to consider after another sacramental encounter in the marital bed, 'whither hire thoughte it paradys or helle' (l. 1964). We understand how the male's 'paradys terrestre' (l. 1332) may create and be the female's 'helle'. The text which sponsors such reflection never encourages any conventional moral judgements against May as it depicts her desperate attempt to alleviate her subjection to this legalised rape by turning to Damyan. As he did in the *Wife of Bath's Prologue*, Chaucer stimulates reflection on the domination of life and literature by unexamined male assumptions and images:

> By God! if wommen hadde writen stories,
> As clerkes han withinne hire oratories,
> They wolde han writen of men moore wikkednesse

Than al the mark of Adam may redresse.
. . .
The clerk, when he is oold, and may noght do
Of Venus werkes worth his olde sho,
Thanne sit he doun, and writ in his dotage
That wommen kan nat kepe hir mariage!
(*Wife of Bath's Prologue*, ll. 693–6, 707–10)

This male poet cannot of course be substitute for the silenced
voices and buried experience of half the human species: but
his texts can awaken the kind of awareness which is an
essential aspect of the long struggle to challenge and dissolve
the male hegemony which continues to deform the lives of
women *and* men.

The poem's concluding play with mythological deities also
encourages such reflexivity by satirising its absence.
Watching May's attempts to loosen Januarie's enslavement of
her, Pluto complains about the wickedness, the 'untrouthe
and brotilnesse' of women, deploying assorted clichés from
the anti-feminist tradition (ll. 2237–61). In the self-righteous
notes of conventional male wisdom he tells her:

Th'experience so preveth every day
The tresons whiche that wommen doon to man.
(ll. 2238–9)

Chaucer's contexts explode this stance in a burst of ironic
laughter, for he has just told us how the authoritative
speaker had himself 'ravysshed' Proserpyna, fetched her 'in
his grisely carte' and forced her to be his wife in hell (ll.
2225–33)—an obvious image of Januarie's marriage to May.
All too representative of male moralisation, he then has the
gall to complain about women's 'tresons' to men! Chaucer
continues to mock the masculine stance as it expresses
solidarity with the 'honourable knyght', the 'worthy knyght'
Januarie, absolutely certain that it is *simply* because he is

old and blind that May seeks another man (ll. 2252-61). She seeks another man, of course, but because she is miserably locked in a marriage she did not make. Furthermore, the poet exposes the male god's use of the Bible as one centred on the self-righteous maintenance of crude sexism (ll. 2242-51): he does so by allowing the wife a thoroughly cogent refutation of Pluto's 'auctorites' and the use he tries to make of them (ll. 2276-304). Indeed, Chaucer gives the woman the same exegesis and arguments that Prudence offers in her decisive defence of women against traditional anti-feminist cant in the *Tale of Melibee* (ll. 1056, 1069-78). The fact that some scholars try to teach us that the poem is anti-feminist is risible, although such responses would hardly have surprised the poet who writes into his work the Host's mindlessly sexist response to the *Clerk's Tale*.

*   *   *

Before leaving the unhappy subject of Christian marriage and patriarchy under market conditions, we should take up an issue raised earlier in this chapter. Namely, that Chaucer's strictly literary heritage included a certain cult of 'love' evolved in many medieval romances and courtly writings.[12] He certainly knew the contradictory strands in the writings around sexual love produced for European courtly society in the high and later Middle Ages, but his knowledge of such materials tells us nothing of his own assessment and use of them. Perhaps still the most popular image of such writing is that it involved an inversion of traditional power relations between males and females, with the knightly male devotedly serving and obeying the noble lady, seeking her 'mercy' and 'grace' which would finally be granted him. (There still seems an erroneous but widespread assumption among students beginning the study of medieval literature that adultery is an essential component of courtly literature of love, perhaps a legacy of C.S. Lewis's influential *Allegory of Love*.) In so far as this popular image was at least one aspect of the upper-class language of love, the response of a knight, contemporary with Chaucer, is worth quoting:

> These wordes are but sport and esbatement of lordes and of felawes in a language moche comyn...these wordes coste to them but lytyll to say for to gete the better and sooner the grace and good wylle of theyr paramours. For of suche wordes and other moche merveyllous many one vseth full ofte. But how be hit that they saye that for them and for theyr love they done hit, in good feyth, they done it only for to enhaunce them self.[13]

That is, courtly forms are fundamentally a game played out according to rules invented by males for their own self-interest. The judgement in this passage accords with the view of the historian J. Huizinga that in the Middle Ages, 'all the conventions of love are the work of men: even when it dons an idealistic guise, erotic culture is altogether saturated by male egotism.'[14] This generalisation is a good starting-point from which to consider Chaucer's treatment of specifically courtly representations of women and sexual relations.

I shall now concentrate the discussion on a poem considered from another perspective in Chapter 2, the *Knight's Tale*. The poem immediately displays the ground on which male service of women in courtly wooing is constructed. These are presented as organised male violence which precedes the subjugation of women. For the text opens with the observation that Theseus had 'conquered al the regne of Femenye' (l. 866), a victory for the armed forces of the worshipper of Mars. This is the context in which Chaucer sets courtly forms of love and marriage. He also evokes it through Theseus's comment that 'every man/Wol helpe hymself in love', recalling how he himself was 'a servant' in love, enduring 'loves peyne' in the male courtly mode (ll. 1777-8, 1813-17). The ironic dimensions of these comments for their writer are highlighted by recalling how he fills out the allusions in his *House of Fame* and *Legend of Good Women*. In both these poems Theseus symbolises the classic example of male egotism inhabiting the courtly forms of love and service. The key words 'pity', 'service', 'mercy', 'true', recur in these accounts which culminate in the duke's abandonment of the woman he has courted and used, now his wife, on an island inhabited only by wild beasts. The courtly language is presented as a male's medium for manipulating and exploiting the female, a language of power (*Legend of Good Women*, ll. 1886-2227; *House of Fame*, ll. 405-26). The *Knight's Tale* itself unfolds to illuminate and flesh out these allusions.

Emily is introduced in a manner which exemplifies one of the dominant forms in which western men have represented females in literature, visual art and, now, advertising (ll. 1034-79). She is walking in an enclosed garden and more beautiful 'to sene/Than is the lylie upon his stalke grene', 'fressher' than May with its 'floures newe', complexion like 'the rose'—a tissue of conventional images for admirable women in romances, the lily (flower of virginity) fused with the rose (flower of sexual promise). In this conventional set of perceptions the woman exists solely as an object in the male's gaze. Such representation fragments and dehumanises the female human being, reducing her to the terms of seemingly spontaneous yet profoundly conventional male desire and its language. Flowers are objects to be cultivated, gazed at, enjoyed, plucked and cast away at their owner's pleasure. Flowers are passive, do not have subjectivity, do not answer back or run away, do not have any powers to put out against the plucker. They are not an image traditionally used by men to symbolise males they admire. As with modern advertisements, this literary tradition teaches male and females to construct ideals of 'femininity' through the fetishised images of male desire. Images which fragment, reduce and distort full human potentials are projected as images of 'femininity'. To deviate from the models and the roles they prescribe is to be 'un-feminine' and so 'un-attractive', 'odd'. In such texts women are taught to see themselves through the gaze of conventional male fantasies, to define their own sexuality through the eyes of men.

One obvious question might be put here: is Chaucer at this point unselfconsciously and uncritically propagating the traditional set of representations and ideology I have described, or is he making it a topic for reflection? The problems in determining just what an author's 'intentions' were are notoriously difficult. Furthermore, in this case would they have been the same when he first wrote the poem as when he later reworked it into the *Canterbury Tales*? Whatever the answer, it seems to me that the text itself, as a whole, systematically makes the forms in which the woman is represented and celebrated a topic for critical reflection, working more subtly and deeply than the treatment of courtly love in the *Legend of Good Women* and *House of Fame*, but working from a similar ironic stance. This, I hope, the discussion above and below will support.

Chaucer follows the traditional presentation of 'feminin-ity' with the knights' gazing ('hurt right now thurghout myn ye', 'hir beautee hurte hym', ll. 1096, 1114), and their decision to 'love' Emily and 'serve' her. Whether she be 'womman or goddesse' unless they have 'hir mercy and hir grace' they will die (ll. 1095–151)—all thoroughly con-ventional and all part of the vision of women as passive objects whose sole fulfilment and glory is to gratify male desire. The text then decisively 'places' these conventional images and protestations of male service and courtly loving. For as the knights decide they cannot *both* love and serve the lily-rose on whom they have been gazing, their friendship turns into hatred on a rivalry to possess the flower/woman in the garden. To neither man are the woman's feelings or wishes relevant. Conditioned by the perception of woman reflected in their language, they never attribute any subjectivity to her, never imagine a mind and will independent of male fantasies and desires. As Arcite reflects on their current state as prisoners he is made to disclose the reality of the sexual relations underlying the rhetoric of goddesses, or of precious flowers, the rhetoric of humble male service and love:

> We stryve as dide the houndes for the boon;
> They foughte al day, and yet hir part was noon.
> Ther cam a kyte, whil that they were so wrothe,
> And baar awey the boon bitwixe hem bothe.
> (ll. 1177–80)

The bone is a fragment of a dead body, consumed by predatory creatures. It presents the woman, dehumanised and transformed by male representations and practices; the hound and kite figure the devoted male lovers. (Perhaps the image will recall for some readers the Jewish myth, sanctified in the Christian Bible, that Woman was made out of Man's rib!) The image penetrates to the heart of the courtly 'erotic culture' and in doing so rather supports Huizinga's contention that it was 'saturated by male egotism'.

Nothing in the long poem qualifies this judgement. The goddess Emily is a mere object whose fate is decided by males in their exercise of military violence—the males agree 'to darreyne hire by bataille' (ll. 1609, 1853). This fusion of male desire and violence offers further insight into conventional male sexuality. It suggests how inter-male competitiveness and machismo can be conventionally displaced into heterosexual 'love'—the male battle for power being fought over the subjected body of the woman. Male

79

desire for the woman is actually increased and made obsessive by the knowledge that another man competes for her. (This, as we shall see, is a syndrome Chaucer also displayed in Diomede's desire for Criseyde: *Troilus and Criseyde*, V.ll. 74-105, 141-75.)

Here, as in his treatment of the Wife of Bath and May, Chaucer explicitly guides the reader's imagination to reflect on the way male traditions have 'written out' female subjectivity, negated it. For he gives Emily an expression of her own desire (ll. 2304-30). She wishes to be free from men. Praying to Diana she states her wish to 'be no love ne wyf', and

> to walken in the wodes wilde,
> And noght to ben a wyf and be with childe.
> Noght wol I knowe compaignye of man.
>
> (see ll. 2304-2311)

She wants neither Palamon nor Arcite, praying for 'love and pees bitwixe hem two' and that their 'hoote love and hir desir' be quenched. But no one else thinks a woman, goddess though she may be, should have a being autonomous of male will, so no one consults her.

Quite the contrary: and when the attempt 'to darreyne hire by bataille' ends in confusion, her fate is determined by Theseus's political designs, discussed in Chapter 2 (ll. 2967-80, 3067-89). Chaucer's text continues to subvert the pretensions of courtly discourses of love right up to its conclusion. Theseus sends for Emily and Palamon to hear his parliamentary oration in the service of Athenian political expansionism. He tells her that he and his Parliament, her all-male rulers, have decided that she is to marry Palamon. Hilariously enough, Chaucer has the Duke use the conventional courtly language of love and male devotion or service to women in a context where the full apparatus of patriarchal power in the public and private spheres is being displayed. Theseus instructs Emily to have pity and bestow her 'grace' on Palamon, 'youre owene knyght/That serveth yow': the fact that Emily never invited or wanted such 'service', nor the actual content of such 'service', are issues that cannot find place in Theseus's discourse. He tells her to reward this (unsolicited) 'service' with 'wommanly pitee' and 'gentil mercy'. By giving these words to the ruler in this context, Chaucer invites us to reflect just how totally such a language fixing or defining female virtues is the product of *male* self-interest and manipulation (ll. 3075–89). Its pretence to some impersonal, 'high' moral ground is decisively exposed by the text's particulars and the overall movement we have followed. Emily stands silent: deprived of language, of will, of any autonomy. The poem closes in conventional romance jollity, with a marriage agreed 'By al the conseil and the baronage' (l. 3096)—bliss, perfect bliss, for both male *and* female, of course!

The romance closure allows readers to abandon the sharp and sustained critical perspectives of the poem, to luxuriate in a few lines which image what most readers doubtless fancy—a life of 'alle wele', 'blisse', 'richesse' and 'heele' enjoyed in an utterly uncomplicated, undisturbed manner with a 'tendrely' loving spouse (ll. 3101–7). If one's abandonment to this is total, it will probably shape any re-reading of the text, muffling and marginalising the profoundly critical dimensions outlined above and in Chapter 2. But these lines should be taken in the context of the whole, and one's enjoyment of the image they hold up need not involve a suspension of critical intelligence. For one thing, the image in itself, however pleasurable, is a hopelessly inadequate one for sustaining any thought about the nature of long-term, loving relationships and the many kinds of pressures these come under in two peoples' lives, then or today. And for another, as we have seen, the text simply gives one no signs of any positive relationship, let alone mutual love, between Emily and Palamon before Theseus's political decree and the ensuing marriage. Quite the opposite is the case, with the male language and forms of 'love' offering no grounds for any kind of optimism about the possibility of mutual 'blisse' in such marriages.

It is worth noting that Chaucer's art includes a more comic treatment of the discourse of courtly loving than the critical perspectives evolved in the *Knight's Tale*. The comedy often works by invoking courtly language and then foregrounding the physical areas of human experience that its high idiom seeks to sublimate. These processes are plainly illustrated through, for example, the *Miller's Tale*. As most comment-aries on this poem show, in its contrasting idiom it is carefully organised to parallel and echo the *Knight's Tale*, structurally, thematically and in verbal details. It is designed to 'quite' the *Knight's Tale* (ll. 3119–27). Chaucer constantly evokes romance and courtly idioms, especially through the language of the parish clerk, Absolon—through descriptions of his appearance, his aspirations and his behaviour as a would-be courtly lover, a petit-bourgeois Palamon. As soon as he evokes such noble discourse, however, Chaucer clashes it mockingly with a very different idiom. For example, after describing his 'love-longynge' and in preparation for his courting, Absolon determines:

> I wol go slepe an houre or tweye,
> And al the nyght thanne wol I wakke and pleye,
> (ll. 3685–6)

As Charles Muscatine observed, courtly lovers never need to catch up on lost sleep. So the laugh is on the inept Absolon. But the laughter cuts both ways, against the courtly fictions too. For the lines point to the areas of human experience the elevated romances dissolve and so to the comic distortions in the models of humanity they generate. The poetry works in a similar way when Absolon acknowledges he sweats (l. 3703)—how absurdly uncourtly: but also, we reflect, what an absurd and laughably pretentious tradition that must be which obscures such bodily function altogether. The poem is replete with this double-faced comedy, and it culmintates in the concluding episodes involving the woman and the rival males. Absolon kneels before the lady's window and pleads: 'Lemman, thy grace, and sweete bryd thyn oore!' (l.3726). Here is the language and posture of the male in the courtly lyric and romance, devotedly begging the woman for grace and mercy. The poet then clashes this with a very different idiom:

> 'Have do,' quod she, 'com of, and speed the faste,
> Lest that oure neighbores thee espie'
> (ll.3728-9)

Like the noble Palamon and Arcite, Absolon's version of 'love' is predatory and based on fragmenting the female to fit the reductive fantasies of conventional male desire (c.f. ll.3346-47 with Arcite's image of the hounds, the bone and the kite, *Knight's Tale*, ll.1177-80). For this the fastidious clerk gets his reward:

> Derk was the nyght as pich, or as the cole,
> And at the wyndow out she putte hir hole,
> And Absolon, hym fil no bet ne wers,
> But with his mouth he kiste hir naked ers
> Ful savourly, er he were war of this.
> Abak he stirtes, and thoughte it was amys,
> For wel he wiste a womman hath no berd.
> He felte a thyng al rough and long yherd,
> And seyd, 'Fy! allas! what have I do?'
>   'Tehee!' quod she, and clapte the wyndow to. . .
> (ll.3731-40)

Both the high courtly idiom *and* its inept imitation objectivise
the woman into an assortment of desirable 'bits'. And while
the mockery of Absolon is obvious enough, we should not
miss the inclusion of the genuine courtly performance in the
writing's satiric scope. This is not only manifested in the
similarity with which women are perceived in the two
idioms. It is also, once more, shown by foregrounding the
physical, the 'naked ers', in a manner which encourages us to
consider the peculiar absences in the courtly and romance
representations of human being. Its sublimations of the
physical, especially of the upper-class body, are brought to
attention and mocked in the carnival world of this fabliau.

The poem's conclusion works in a similar way. Alison's
lover hears his rival begging for a kiss, and expressing needs
courtly people are apparently above, gets up 'for to pisse'—
rhyming the words 'kisse' and 'pisse' Chaucer suggests how
conventional language may compartmentalise our areas of
experience in ways which can systematically distort the self-
images we project to each other (ll.3792–8). Now instead of
the upper-class tournament we have Nicholas sticking his
'ers' out of the window, 'Over the buttok, to the haunch-
bon' and waiting for his rival's mouth. Absolon approaches,
addressing, as he thinks, the lady:

> 'Spek, sweete bryd, I noot nat where thou art.'
> This Nicholas anon leet fle a fart
> As greet as it had been a thonder-dent
> That with the strook he was almost yblent.
>
> (ll.3805–8)

This stroke is immediately repaid, not with upper-class
means of violence, of course, but with hot iron onto Nichol-
arse's naked 'ers':

> Of gooth the skyn an hande-brede aboute

84

The hoote kultour brende so his toute
(ll.3809–12)

Again, as the poem closes in its carnivalesque version of the flood and Last Judgement, we see how this episode in the lovers' conflict generates a critical perspective on courtly modes of writing and practice. It evokes their *similarity* to the down-town version of them while also suggesting central areas of our embodied living that they consistently obscure and sublimate. The same processes can be followed in the *Nun's Priest's Tale* (for example, ll.2859–95, 3157–86), but I shall now move on.

*   *   *

And that is to consider those texts which illustrate the most positive versions of love and sexuality in Chaucer's work. The *Franklin's Tale* still mainly seems to be taught in our sixth forms as Chaucer's resolution of 'the marriage debate' in *The Canterbury Tales*, as a poem celebrating the successful fusion of love and marriage in an ideal which is the genial author's. There is undoubtedly much about this reading that is attractive and humane; nor is the text lacking in passages which encourage it. The poem, after all, opens with an admirable attempt to express an ideal of marriage as a non-coercive, freely-chosen, mutual relationship, which, as we have seen, was very far from 'normal' in fourteenth-century Europe. Indeed, in Chaucer's contexts the ideal seems utopian, and the poet signals this by setting his tale in a non-Christian land where the woman Dorigen is quite free from economic pressures or patriarchal power of any kind. It is to be a fiction which explores the horizons of con-temporary forms of language and practice, seeking to press beyond them.

The poet has the male renounce all traditional forms of

domination, except the public appearance of 'soveraynetee' (ll.729–52). On these grounds the couple get married. This is followed by a memorable though complex passage attempting to express the need for both female and male 'libertee' in genuinely loving relationships:

> Love is a thyng as any spirit free.
> Wommen, of kynde, desiren libertee,
> And nat to been constreyned as a thral;
> And so doon men, if I sooth seyen shal.
> (ll.767–71)

Love and domination, 'maistrye', are quite incompatible (ll.764–6). The text is stressing that loving relationships must be grounded in the *independent* strengths and wishes of lovers who quite freely choose to live together and nourish their love. Both men and women 'desiren libertee' but, the passage goes on to argue, such liberty is perfectly compatible with long-lasting stable relationships. If, that is, both people love with intelligence, patience and mutual 'suffrance', freely-chosen forebearance (ll.771–90). This is an impressive model and could, perhaps, reflect ideals that inform Chaucer's own critical treatment of conventional forms of sexuality and their languages.

Nevertheless, the *Franklin's Tale* itself does not show us the realisation of this ideal. Arveragus, the knightly husband, leaves Dorigen and the 'blisse' and 'joye' of their marriage to pursue his own militaristic 'honour' but the text gives us no sign that there has been any discussion, let alone mutality, in the decision (ll.803–18). This silence may suggest the betrayal of the ideal formulated at the poem's opening, but in itself is obviously not decisive. The same cannot be said about the husband's performance at the poem's climax.

Before treating this important episode, however, it seems worth pointing out that the poem also contains another critical representation of courtly forms of male loving, quite in accord with the perspectives which inform the *Knight's Tale*, discussed earlier in this chapter. Aurelius uses the love-languages and rituals of male 'servyce' and friendship to persuade Dorigen to make love with him (ll.925–1068). The wife is unequivocal in her response, telling him, 'shal I nevere been untrewe wyf'; she orders him: 'Lat swiche folies out of youre herte slyde' (ll.984,1002). Her whole being is *freely* faithful to a man who is 'hire housbonde and hire love also' (l.922), as the poem emphasises. In his absence it is he the woman longs for (ll.818–21, 888–94, 919–24). She fears for his safety dreading the 'grisly feendly rokkes blake' (ll.857–94) and it is this fear she lets surface in her rejection of the courtly Aurelius. If he performs the impossible task of removing every single rock along the coast that threatens her husband's safety, she tells him only then would she be his 'love' (ll.989–98). Next she unambiguously says that she knows this will never happen and tells him to forget such 'folies' (ll.1001–2). In the event it turns out that Dorigen has rather foolishly underestimated the depths of male egotism pervading the courtly forms of love. Instead of accepting the reality of her subjectivity, her autonomy and her love for her husband, Aurelius pays a conjuror to create an illusion that the rocks have vanished. He then pretends to have removed the rocks, claiming that he acts humbly, out of 'love' for his 'sovereyn lady', for her 'honour', doing what she 'commanded' him to do (ll.1308–38). She should, therefore, make love with him. This is wonderful self-deception for she actually commanded him to dismiss such 'folies' and made her own desires clear enough. But the poet's satiric target is not one squire: rather it is the manipulative nature of the male language of 'servyce' and 'love', a language which certainly has its modern equivalents.

Dorigen is psychologically paralysed at the mess she now feels herself to be in. Not surprisingly, she is quite unable to make any critical judgement of the male's claims and language (ll.1339–458). Her passivity seems total. She does nothing until her husband returns and asks her why she is so miserable (ll.1459–61). Presenting the situation to him she encounters yet another example of self-righteous egotism couched in a language proclaiming only service of 'Trouthe' and 'verray love' of the woman (ll.1474–9). He instructs his wife that she owes it to 'Trouthe' to allow this man to 'screw' her (to call sexual acts that are not free expressions of mutual love 'making love' seems a bad misuse of language). It is worth noting that readers do not always recognise the stupidity of this position, let alone its immorality. But Chaucer certainly did.[15] In his *Tale of Melibee* he has the moralist Prudence teach that if someone promises something but breaks that promise in a 'juste cause' he is morally justified. If the original vow is 'dishonest', or 'may nat goodly be parfourned or kept', then it *must* be broken. If this position is denied, 'thilke counseil is wikked' (ll.1064–6, 1225–30). *Melibee* is certainly written in a different literary genre, but in this case at least Chaucer's romance invites us, in this very different mode, to move towards similar moral understanding. Arveragus's 'conseil' is undoubtedly 'wikked'. It ignores the prior 'truth' Dorigen explicitly drew to Aurelius's attention—the freely chosen truth to her husband and their marriage. It ignores the full context of Dorigen's response to Aurelius which was described above. It even fails to examine Aurelius's false claims to have removed all the rocks. It also commands Dorigen to carry out an action that violates her own sense of truth and demands that she unwillingly subject herself to Aurelius. In relation to the aspirations of their marriage, his decision is disastrous. For all the intentions to create a relationship of mutuality and freedom from domination Arveragus never pauses to find out Dorigen's feelings, wishes or ideas. In this crisis the woman's subjectivity and desire is denied by her husband.

She stands before his judgement deprived of voice. These facts are stressed in the conclusion Chaucer gives the husband:

> But with that word he brast anon to wepe,
> And seyde, 'I yow forbede, up peyne of deeth,
> That nevere, whil thee lasteth lyf ne breeth,
> To no wyght telle thou of this aventure,—
> As I may best, I wol my wo endure
>
> (ll.1480–6)

This is pretty ghastly. The husband threatens to kill his wife if she lets anyone know of the misery he now condemns her to endure. His public reputation as a 'manly' husband seems uppermost in his mind—this may recall his wish to keep the public marks of 'soveraynetee' in his egalitarian marriage. All the alleged transcendence of crude male domination collapses into this display of unregenerate egotism apparently devoid of affection and care for the woman. It is *she* who will have to endure the violation of unwilling sexual intercourse, rape. The knight is consumed with self-centred orientation—'As *I* may best, *I* wol *my* wo endure.' Without reply, Dorigen obeys, going off to endure Aurelius's sexual actions. It seems 'soveraynetee' is more than an external mask. The projected ideal fails.

But the text does not finish there. When Aurelius meets the passive and utterly miserable Dorigen he is suddenly converted. He feels 'compassioun' for her and decides that to rape her now would be 'a cherlyssh wrecchednesse /Agayns franchise and alle gentillesse' (ll.1499–524). So he frees her. Hearing about this act, the conjuror waives the squire's ruinous financial debt to him, inspired to do 'a gentil dede' (ll.1557–620). As for the husband and wife, the narrative informs us that they now lived in 'blisse': 'Nevere eft ne was ther angre hem bitwene', he 'cherisseth hire as though she were a queene', and she is 'trewe for evermoore' (ll.1551–5). This is the same kind of 'blissful' romance ending as that found in the *Knight's Tale*, discussed earlier in the chapter. It too allows what I take to be a naive reading. Namely, one in which assertions about how they all lived happily ever after in untroubled bliss are received with such contentment that the reader suspends his or her critical powers. He or she then fails to reflect on the problematic relations between the overall movements of the poem and the claims it makes at its close. Not that such a 'naive' reading is worthless. Like the 'happy ending' itself, it affirms that people may be able to break the destructive bonds of egotism, becoming capable of generous responses to the independent needs and desires of another, even when these conflict with their own wishes. In doing so it may, perhaps, encourage such responsiveness. Certainly it affirms an optimistic image of human possibilities, one that, however utopian, is necessary if people are to strive for à social order with happier human relationships than those Chaucer's art tends to display.

Nevertheless, I think it is better to combine this 'naive' reading with a far less happy one. (Nor is disenchantment the same as despair.) We should not ignore the fact that between the grisly collapse of the marital ideal and the final affirmations in the 'happy ending', the text gives us absolutely no processes of regeneration—Averagus and Dorigen are absent. Yet questions about processes of regeneration are too central to evade. How can people turn forms of being that are destructive into ones that may enable the fulfilment of happier human potentials? How can internal and external drives towards tragedy be transformed in both personal and collective spheres? (This question seems to have been at least one motivation in Shakespeare's turning from the tragedies to the late plays, especially *The Winter's Tale*.) The 'happy ending' of the *Franklin's Tale* simply ignores these issues. Such an absence means that we have no grounds for any faith whatsoever in the final assertions. Indeed, it serves rather to foster a scepticism towards these assertions, highlighting their imposed and arbitrary nature, focusing on them as a depressingly superficial evasion of major problems the text has generated. This reading would see the conventional romance ending of the poem as exemplifying how such closures can suppress intelligence and imaginative attention to the difficulties in realising visions of a more fulfilling human future. It would find the 'naive' reading an inadequate surrender to fantasies of transcendence which are simply not grounded in the processes created in the text. The more unhappy consciousness fostered by the reading I have been proposing could persuade us to retreat into a stoical individualism cultivating the kind of resignation we see in some of Chaucer's own short poems (as the ballad 'Truth'). This would see the overall movement of the text as including an ironic, disenchanting subversion of its utopian moments and the very ideals espoused by the married couple at its opening. But a pessimistic reading which has an unhappy grasp of the destructive forces dramatised in the poem can still be wedded to a fully conscious optimism of the will, a will to strive for a world (within and without) where the vision of free and yet stable love might, perhaps, be realised, a vision through which present degradations can be more sharply perceived, criticised and, perhaps, only perhaps, overcome.

From this discussion of the *Franklin's Tale* it will be clear that I no longer find much point in continuing attempts to discriminate the formal pilgrim-narrator, the Franklin, from his creator, Chaucer. As observed before, *The Canterbury Tales* manifest no consistent commitment to a psychologically 'realistic' and consistent pilgrim-narrator whose identity determines the fiction and in terms of whose 'personality' the fiction should be interpreted as a 'projection'. The narrative strategies of one poem differ from those of another, and within one text the formal narrative voice often fragments into markedly contrasting voices, while parts of different poems, attributed to different tellers, manifest the same narrative voice. To reiterate a point made earlier: there is no reason to seek kinds of coherence or consistency the texts do not have and which the author had no interest in achieving. As for questions about how Chaucer himself read the *Franklin's Tale*, plainly enough we do not know. Nor should we assume that if he re-read it in different contexts its meaning would have remained stable. These are interpretative questions about which he himself was acutely conscious (as we noted in Chapter 1). Certainly the poem disqualifies any attempt to maintain what I have called a 'naive' reading as it explores major issues in our culture in the complex manner I have attempted to describe.

* * *

Before turning to *Troilus and Criseyde* I wish to mention the model of a courtly woman which Chaucer created in an early work, *The Book of the Duchess*. This contrasts sharply with Emily, Dorigen and that figure who tries to take control of her life, the Wife of Bath. In *The Book of the Duchess* Blanche is represented as retaining decisive initiative in her relationships both before and after marriage (ll.817–1041, 1088–111, 1171–297). She has all the ideal 'feminine' courtly graces but the poet shows her refusing to exist as an object in the male gaze. Males gaze and attempt to construct her look to fit their manipulative courtly language of 'mercy' (examined above), but Blanche rejects them. The men are 'fooles' for trying to impose on her, for as to her looking:

Hyt nas no countrefeted thyng;

Hyt was hir owne pure lokyng
(ll.869–70)

Her own version of 'grace' is not the one we have seen
courtly males deploying: it is part of her own 'stedefast
perseveraunce' (l.1006–7). Nor is she a flower owned,
cultivated and plucked by males. She has 'wyt', 'reson', free
will, and she exercises these in her living (ll.921–2, 1010–
14). Her existence is not totally determined by the courtly
discourses and practises moulding sexual relations into
images of unreflexive male desire. These are rejected as
'knakkes smale' (ll.1015–33). Out of this form of being she
is able to marry a knight in a relationship where she is
represented as maintaining her own identity and subjectivity, unlike Dorigen.

This may be an impressive model with which to think
about the cultivation of female independence and how this
can be maintained within a loving and stable relationship. It
addresses the same problems Chaucer faced in the *Franklin's
Tale* but concentrates on the feminine strengths necessary
for the development of a mutual love free from traces of
domination. Nevertheless, the model is an abstractly
idealised one, attributed to the memory of the husband
lamenting his now dead wife. The literary mode presents the
woman and her married relationship in a manner which
delivers them from the pressures of history and specific
society under exclusively male control. It is a mode
appropriate for sketching in a platonic ideal. But its evasion
of the forces of determinate historical circumstances is also
its limitation as a model and as an imaginative engagement
with the issues involved. In *Troilus and Criseyde* Chaucer
created a text which includes the ideals represented through
Blanche, but goes far beyond them in its engagement with
human sexuality and its confrontation of the forces he had
bracketed in *The Book of the Duchess*.

Troilus and Criseyde, perhaps the most profound love poem in English, goes beyond the horizons of medieval (and most later) literature. It generates a complex and delicate exploration of female consciousness immersed in a society organised by men where the cultural forms, in Huizinga's words, quoted earlier, are 'altogether saturated by male egotism'. In his creation of Criseyde and the extensive reflections he gives her, Chaucer produces a brilliant meditation on the ways in which one's consciousness and the most intimate areas of being are shaped by contemporary social organisation and dominant ideologies, even when their effects are unambiguously destructive. The poem achieves memorable insights to the interactions between the joyful potentials of sexual love, so powerfully represented, and the collective organisation of living often known as 'civilisation'.

Troilus and Criseyde includes an extensive critique of the forms of courtly wooing already considered in this chapter. Troilus in the first two books, Pandarus throughout, and Diomede in the final book, all display the exploitatory male language of courtly 'service', 'worship', 'friendship' and 'love'. Chaucer's satirical perspective here is never in doubt. For example, he gives Diomede the full courtly language of worshipful service, selfless friendship, obedient love and prayers for mercy and grace—at great length (V,ll.85–175, 918–45). This is juxtaposed with the observation that the man's aim was to 'net' Criseyde, and that, 'To fisshen hire, he leyde out hook and lyne' (V,ll.771–7). This juxtaposition forcefully symbolises the essential degradation of women in the conventional discourse and practice of male courtship. Furthermore, Chaucer again makes explicit a factor he treated in the *Knight's Tale*—heterosexual desire in such a culture becomes a displacement of competition between males seeking to display their own machismo and virtuosity to each other. So Criseyde becomes more desirable to

Diomede because he knows Troilus loves her (V,ll.74–105, 792–8). He comments:

> whoso myghte wynnen swich a flour
> From hym for whom she morneth nyght and day,
> He myghte seyn he were a conquerour.
>
> (V.ll.793–5)

'Love' becomes a competition for the possession of women between males competing for power and prestige: to 'conquer' a woman is to 'conquer' another man, doubly bolstering the male ego. It is also worth noticing how Chaucer 'places' the traditional love language in which the woman is represented by males as a flower, thus revealing its essentially reductive and predatory meaning. He did the same in the *Knight's Tale* in a passage discussed in detail earlier in this chapter.

Nevertheless the poem also shows that someone who begins from the familiar language and practices of courtly 'love' may be able to move through and beyond these. This is what happens to Troilus, and one of the pleasures of this text is following the uneven processes of the transformation across the first three books. This transformation makes possible the achievement of a relationship beyond the horizons of the conventional language with which it was evolved and without which it would be unimaginable. For one factor here is that Troilus comes to take the surface forms of courtly discourse so seriously that his living gives them meanings they cannot habitually carry. This is evident in the way that courtly cant about male 'service' eventually comes to have some literal meaning in Troilus's relationship with Criseyde. We see this as part of the gradual overcoming of self-hood, inextricably bound up with the man's recognition late in Book III that Criseyde does have an autonomous subjectivity.

His behaviour in Book IV witnesses to this development. After the Trojan Parliament has determined to trade Criseyde to the Greek army, Troilus, miserably facing the consequences this has for his lover and himself, is given simple advice by Pandarus: 'help thiself anon', 'manly sette the world on six and sevene', snatch Criseyde and rush away from Troy without consulting the woman's wishes (IV,ll.582–630). This exemplifies the habitual 'manly' attitudes underlying the language of service and love. Troilus himself, despite his own protestations, had been quite happy to deceive Criseyde in a manner which played on her well-justified fears about her position as a traitor's daughter, to pressurise her with a lie about his causes for sexual jealousy and to do this in the middle of the night in Pandarus's house after she had been told of his absence (I,ll.1401–750; III,ll.750–1057). But by Book IV he has opened himself to Criseyde, renouncing the will to dominate: love 'altered his spirit so withinne' (III,l.1778). Now he is able to reject Pandarus's advice on the grounds that this would be another case of 'ravysshyng of wommen'. He decides he will not impose anything on her: whatever his wishes he will do nothing 'but if hireself it wolde' (IV,ll.540–50, 561–7, 631–7). This is the effect of Troilus's 'conversion' in love, the product of the 'newe qualitee' of being he attains in Book III (III,l.1654).

At the same time, Chaucer has Criseyde show intelligence, reflexive powers and desires that have a life quite independent of the competing males. Indeed, in a manner often missed by those who try to construct Criseyde to fit received stereotypes of 'femininity', the poet gives her a capacity for self-reflexivity beyond any he attributes to the male figures (for example, II, ll.598–931, III, ll.981–1057). She is shown organising her desires in a world where all the initiatives (sexual, political, social, economic) are in the hands of armed males and where she is vulnerable as a traitor's daughter.[16] The language she uses in Book II forms a highly intelligent, sensitive meditation on the painful risks run in opening oneself out in love of another, as well as on the risk of losing her identity in marriage and the real risks she now runs by being the object of the king's son's desires (II, ll.771–84, 750–5, 701–14). Through these meditations she 'wex somewhat able to converte', and decides to take the risks, to let the relationship evolve, 'by proces' (II, ll.903, 678). With a marvellously detailed attention to movements of her consciousness the poetry represents this 'process' in Books II and III, always locating it firmly within the limiting social and cultural circumstances.

Despite the problems created by these limits and the manipulative egotism of the males, Criseyde and Troilus grow towards a mutual confidence, into security ('sikernesse'). This process culminates in Book III's magnificent affirmation of sexual union as the expression of their love. (Here again the most intelligent and sensitive forms of language and initiative are attributed to the woman [III, l.981–1057, 1126–34, 1177–87, 1209–11].) The poetry, transcending the degradation of sexuality in the dominant discourses of Chaucer's culture, evokes and celebrates the lovers' gratification as together they 'Felten in love the grete worthynesse' (especially III, ll.1205–318). Criseyde and Troilus create an oasis of 'hevene blisse', of 'perfit joi' which seems to involve the whole human being, body, affections, imagination, intelligence (III, ll.1128–820).

But as we celebrate the poet's achievement and the joy he represents we also know that this *is* a secret oasis. As such it certainly is an escape from the destructive society within which the lovers live; but also, ironically, it is partly generated by that very society. The form of relationship in the oasis is effected, indeed shaped, by the society it seeks to escape. In withdrawal it succumbs to that from which it seeks to withdraw. For the relationship is privatised, unable to break into society, unable to challenge the dominant values, including the militaristic and unreflective male values so alien to those created by the lovers. In agreeing that the relationship should be kept hidden in a secret oasis the lovers also affirm the society and culture which *marginalises* and *downgrades* the values of love such as that evoked in Book III.

It is the culture and society dominated by militaristic commitments and male power which smashes up the oasis, the union between Criseyde and Troilus. The last two books of the poem carefully and clearly show this.[17] Book IV highlights the male aggression and continuous legalised violence which is war—a war, as Troilus reminds Pandarus, triggered off by the rape of a woman (IV, ll.29–321, 547–8). It is men alone who decide that Criseyde should be treated as a commodity and exchanged for Antenor, now a prisoner (IV, ll.141–217). No one thinks her wishes even worth considering. 'Only' a woman, she has no existence in a man's world except as an object of sexual consumption or as a commodity to be traded in what the Trojan males consider their best self-interest. Hector had promised Criseyde protection and he protests, 'We usen here no wommen for to selle': but he is overruled by his fellows (IV, 181; cf. I, ll.92–126). The interactions between the intimate areas of one's being and the wider social contexts within which one develops could not be more sharply exemplified.

Hearing that she is to be sent to live with the Greek army, Criseyde, reasonably enough, despairs, reaffirming the intensity of her love for Troilus (IV, ll.659–79, 731–871). Troilus too had despaired but, as we noticed, he is prepared to rebel and elope with Criseyde if she will agree. He now knows that if their love and sexual union are to survive they must defy 'good' society, its customs and rulers: the oasis is no dwelling-place (IV, ll.1500–26). But Criseyde has not the confident independence of the ruling-class male, and in describing how she rejects his rebellious plan Chaucer shows the force of conventional social ideologies as individuals internalise these and their definition of reality. The woman places the importance of the insane male war (based on the rape of women) above her and Troilus's love. She rejects his plan, protesting:

> But that ye speke, awey thus for to go
> And leten alle youre frendes, God forbede,
> For any womman, that ye sholden so!
> (IV, ll.1555–7)

Unable to attain a critical perspective on the public world and its war, she exhibits a contempt for her own sex and desires which echoes that of the male Parliament. This decisive episode illustrates how secure dominant groups can remain as long as they manage to get subordinate groups to accept degrading self-images and to accept their own values. Criseyde's obedience to her male rulers in Book IV seals her 'fate'. It is in this light we should reinterpret Troilus's and Chaucer's own comments on 'fate' and 'fortune', for the poem itself shows how this is a socially imposed, man-made 'fate'. We do not need any obscure metaphysical concepts to understand the disastrous processes here, however fascinated Chaucer himself was by the metaphysical arguments.

Once removed to the Greek camp Criseyde is totally isolated. With good cause she is terrified, conscious of the threat of rape, 'With wommen fewe, among the Grekis stronge', longing for Troilus and painfully conscious 'that she was allone and hadde nede/Of frendes help' (V, ll.688–749, 1026–7). Nothing in Chaucer's representations of her situation allows readers anything other than the sharpest sense of the overwhelming pressures she is now subject to. It is in these circumstances, so fully realised, that the inevitable male appears to exploit them and the woman, 'To fisshen hire' (V, l.771–7). Having already discussed the poet's treatment of Diomede's language, his 'friendship' and 'love', there is no need to go over that again. Miserably, with self-disgust and yet resignation, Criseyde accommodates to the new man-made reality into which she has been pitched, and gradually accepts Diomede, recognising that reunion with Troilus is never going to be allowed (V, ll.1051–85). Her circumstances are harsh and her whole training as a woman has been in accommodation to the male-dominated world. Anything other than a drift into Diomede's net would have required a quite heroic inner strength which is rare enough anywhere and unimaginable here. Chaucer's writing creates conflicting movements of consciousness and feelings as Criseyde yields herself, now trapped in a web of circumstances she had not chosen (V, ll.841–1085):

> Ther made nevere woman moore wo
> Than she, whan that she falsed Troilus
> (V, ll.1052–3)

Desperately, she tries to accept the loss that has been forced on her and make a stable relationship with the predatory Diomede:

> But syn I se ther is no bettre way,
> And that to late is now for me to rewe,
> To Diomede algate I wol be trewe.
> (V, ll.1069–71)

This is pitiful, and our response in the contexts Chaucer has created should be a sadness grounded in a rich understanding of the destructive role of the social and ideological contexts Chaucer's work has figured so fully.

The male who is strong enough to suggest rebellion against 'good' society turns out to have undergone such a total 'conversion' that he refuses to 'unloven' Criseyde, whatever the outcome:

> ...I se that clene out of youre mynde
> Ye han me cast; and I ne kan nor may,
> For al this world, withinne myn herte fynde
> To unloven yow a quarter of a day!
>
> (V, ll.1695–8)

The passionate fidelity of this love is an image of the very constancy of human love which the poem's epilogue seeks to deny as a possibility among humans (V, ll.1828–69). In reading the pious declamations of the epilogue we must recall that the overall narrative and the poetry's minute particulars have disclosed how the union between Criseyde and Troilus was *not* destroyed by generalised human 'sin', or an inevitable 'transcience', or 'mutability', or frivolous 'vanity'. As I have observed, and as pursuit of the given textual references will confirm, the delicate specificity with which the work creates the processes of love is sustained in its exploration of the intolerable social forces which destroy the lovers' union. The work as a whole includes a marvellous celebration of sexual love and gratification, holding up a 'utopian' image of joy and freedom against which we judge the civilised 'reality' which undermines and destroys this happiness. Whatever Chaucer's own readings of the epilogue, however divided his own responses may have been, divisions probably reflected in his *Retractions* to *The Canterbury Tales*, the poem as a whole encourages us to reject the generalised incantations and moralistic clichées with which it responds to the final tragedy. It should help to recognise the epilogue as a language in which no serious psychological, moral and social exploration is possible.[18]

Readers will judge these comments on the epilogue and its relations to the long, very subtle poem which precedes it, from their own experiences and their own ideology.

Inevitably the grounds of their reading will not be impersonal, perfectly objective nor simply transcending their own social and cultural moment. It will include their own sexual relations, their own models of human potential, their own fears, defeats and projects. As argued in the first chapter, even the most devotedly 'historicist' reader, which we should all strive to be, reads from her or his own present, recontextualising the text in a field which is the site of vital human struggles over present and future forms of living.

Notes

Chapter 1

1. For example: R. Brenner, 'Agrarian class structure and economic development in pre-industrial Europe', *Past and Present*, 70 (1976), 30–75; R. Brenner, 'The agrarian roots of European capitalism', *Past and Present*, 97 (1982), 16–113; F.R.H. Du Boulay, *An Age of Ambition* (Nelson, 1970); G. Duby, *Rural Economy and Country Life in the Medieval West* (Arnold, 1968), pp. 277–8, 283–6, 329–36; R. Hilton, *Bond Men Made Free* (Temple Smith, 1973); R. Hilton, *The English Peasantry in the Later Middle Ages* (Oxford U.P., 1975); R. Hilton, 'Feudalism and the origins of capitalism', *History Workshop*, 1 (1976), 9–25; R.E. Lerner, *The Age of Adversity* (Cornell U.P., 1968); H.A. Miskimin, *The Economy of Early Renaissance Europe* (Prentice-Hall, 1969), pp. 30–51; M. Mollat and P. Wolff, *The Popular Revolutions of the Late Middle Ages* (Allen & Unwin, 1973); R. Bird, *The Turbulent London of Richard II* (Longmans, 1949). There is also the invaluable collection of primary texts edited by R.B. Dobson, *The Peasants' Revolt of 1381* (Macmillan, 1970). On the economy of the period, there is a recent introductory and very accessible survey by J.L. Bolton, *The Medieval English Economy* (Dent, 1980).

2. Bolton, *Medieval English Economy*, pp. 9, 13; Lerner, *The Age of Adversity*, pp. 17, 83.

3. This is another area of medieval culture and orthodox religion too often ignored: see especially the translation from Bernard Gui's Inquisitor's manual in *Heresies of the High Middle Ages*, ed. W.L. Wakefield and A.P. Evans (Columbia U.P., 1969), pp. 373–447. Also: M.D. Lambert, *Medieval Heresy* (Arnold, 1977); G. Leff, *Heresy in the Later Middle Ages*, 2 vols (Manchester U.P., 1967), I, pp. 34–47; B. Hamilton, *The Medieval Inquisition* (Arnold, 1981).

4. B.H. Putnam, *The Enforcement of the Statute of Labourers* (Columbia U.P., 1908), p. 91. On the Church's 'incorporation', see L.K. Little, *Religious Poverty and the Profit Economy in Medieval Europe* (Elek, 1978); R.W. Southern, *Western Society and the Church in the Middle Ages* (Penguin, 1970). See too the illuminating study of 'clerical careerism' in Cheshire and Lancashire during the later Middle Ages by Michael J. Bennett, *Community, Class and Careerism: Cheshire and Lancashire Society in the Age of Sir Gawain and the Green Knight* (Cambridge U.P., 1983), especially Chapter 8.

5. See especially on this subject, G. Leff, *Dissolution of the Medieval Outlook* (Harper & Row, 1976), Chapter 4.

6. M. Foucault, *Language, Counter-Memory, Practice* (Cornell U.P., 1977), see pp. 156–7; T. Eagleton, *Literary Theory* (Blackwell, 1983), p. 211.

7. F. Lentricchia, *After the New Criticism* (Methuen, 1983), p. 207.

8. All quotations of Chaucer are from *The Works of Geoffrey Chaucer*, ed. F.N. Robinson, 2nd edn (Oxford U.P., 1968). References are to the line numbers in this edition. Here see S. Delany, *Chaucer's House of Fame* (Chicago U.P., 1972); A.C. Spearing, *Medieval Dream Poetry* (Cambridge U.P., 1976), Chapter 2; J. Ferster, *Chaucer on Interpretation* (Cambridge U.P., 1985).

9. Leff, *Dissolution*, Chapters 1–2. The links have yet to be seriously examined.

10. *The Poems of Robert Henryson*, ed. H. Wood (Oliver & Boyd, 1965), pp. 17–24.

11. See examples in D. Aers, *Piers Plowman and Christian Allegory* (Arnold, 1975), Chapters 2–3.

Chapter 2

1. For a classic example of this see Book I of Gower's *Vox Clamantis* dealing with the English rising of 1381, translated in E.W. Stockton, *The Major Latin Works of John Gower* (University of Washington, 1962).
2. From a typical enough sermon in *Middle English Sermons*, W.O. Ross (Early English Text Society, o.s. 209, 1940), p. 237.
3. R. Hilton, *Peasants, Knights and Heretics* (Cambridge U.P., 1976), p.8; also R. Hilton, *English Peasantry in the Later Middle Ages* (Oxford U.P., 1975), pp. 64–73. See too, *The Peasants' Revolt*, ed. R.B. Dobson (Macmillan, 1970); J.L. Bolton, *The Medieval English Economy* (Dent, 1980), pp.144–49, 213–18, 261–3. On Langland in this context, D. Aers, *Chaucer, Langland and the Creative Imagination* (Routledge & Kegan Paul, 1980), Chapter 1.
4. J. Mann, *Chaucer and Medieval Estates Satire* (Cambridge U.P., 1973), pp. 17–37.
5. L.K. Little, *Religious Poverty and the Profit Economy* (Elek, 1978), Part II.
6. Ibid., p. 96.
7. See T. Jones, *Chaucer's Knight: the Portrait of a Medieval Mercenary* (Louisiana State U.P., 1980) and Aers's review in *Studies in the Age of Chaucer*, 1982, pp. 169–75.
8. *Summa Theologiae*, II–II, 77.4.
9. Quoting J.H. Fisher, *John Gower* (Methuen, 1965), p. 258. See too, Bolton, *Medieval English Economy*, pp. 272, 283–85.
10. *The Major Latin Works of John Gower*, p. 260. See too, M.J. Bennett, *Community Class and Careerism* (Cambridge U.P., 1983), pp. 13–14, 88, 109–110, 129.
11. See M. Weber, *The Protestant Ethic and the Spirit of Capitalism* (Unwin, 1930).
12. *General Prologue*, ll.279, 283, 459, 253; see Mann, *Chaucer*, pp. 195–7.
13. *City of God*, IV.5 and IV.6.
14. *The Works of John Clanvowe*, ed. V.J. Scattergood (Brewer Press, 1976), pp. 69–70.
15. See R. Neuse, 'The Knight', in J.A. Burrow (ed.), *Chaucer* (Penguin, 1969), 242–63, here p. 250.

16. 'The Complaint of Chaucer to his Purse', 1.24: see M. Schlauch, 'Chaucer's doctrine of kings and tyrants', *Speculum*, 20 (1945), 133–56.
17. For example, R.M. Jordan, *Chaucer and the Shape of Creation* (Harvard U.P., 1967), p. 204; R.B. Burlin, *Chaucerian Fiction* (Princeton, 1977) pp. 140, 143–4. For disenting voices drowned in the medieval establishment's hymns, see E. Salter, *Chaucer* (Arnold, 1962), pp. 37–70, and D. Reiman, 'The real *Clerk's Tale*', *Texas Studies in Literature and Language*, 5 (1963), 356–73.
18. *City of God*, XV.7; XIV.28; XIX.15. (Augustine is not being offered here as a grid through which to read Chaucer.)
19. On this see Reiman's study, cited in note 17.
20. F.R. Scott, 'Chaucer and the parliament of 1386', *Speculum*, 18 (1943), 80–6; M. Schlauch, cited in note 16.
21. A. Tuck, *Richard II and the English Nobility* (Arnold, 1973); G. Holmes, *The Good Parliament* (Oxford U.P., 1975), Chapters 5–6; M. Schlauch, cited in note 16.
22. On these developments see A.S. McGrade, *The Political Thought of William of Ockham* (Cambridge U.P., 1974); M.J. Wilks, *The Problem of Sovereignty in the Later Middle Ages* (Cambridge U.P., 1964), especially pp. 516–29; M.J. Wilks 'Chaucer and the mystical marriage in medieval political thought', *Bulletin of the John Rylands Library*, 44 (1961–1), 489–530.
23. See R.H. Tawney, *Religion and the Rise of Capitalism* (Penguin, 1964), and C.B. Macpherson, *Possessive Individualism* (Oxford U.P., 1964).

Chapter 3

1. L.K. Little, *Religious Poverty and the Profit Economy* (Elek, 1978), p. 202, see also Chapter 12; and R.W. Southern, *Western Society and the Church in the Middle Ages* (Penguin 1970), pp. 288–92.
2. A.L. Kellogg and L.A. Haselmayer, 'Chaucer's Satire and the Pardoner', *PMLA*, 66 (1951), 251–77; R.W. Southern, *Western Society*, pp. 136–43.

3. See K. Thomas, *Religion and the Decline of Magic* (Peregrine, 1978), Chapter 2, and especially an extraordinarily important book overlooked by medieval literary critics: Jacques Toussaert, *Le Sentiment Religieux en Flandre à la fin du Moyen Age* (Plon, Paris, 1963).

4. G. Leff, *Heresy in the Later Middle Ages*, 2 vols (Manchester U.P., 1967), Chapter 8; M.D. Lambert, *Medieval Heresy* (Arnold, 1977), Chapter 15.

5. See Little, *Religious Poverty*, pp. 42–57.

6. G.I. Langmuir, 'The Knight's Tale of Young Hugh of Lincoln', *Speculum*, 47 (1972), 459–82.

7. Consult R. Bainton, *Christian Attitudes towards War and Peace* (Hodder & Stoughton, 1961).

8. R.J. Schoeck, 'Chaucer's Prioress: Mercy and Tender Heart', in *Chaucer Criticism*, ed. R.J. Schoeck and J. Taylor (University of Notre Dame Press, 1960), vol. I, pp. 245–58.

9. See Chapter 4. On the treatment of sources: J.B. Allen, 'The old way and the Parson's way', *Journal of Medieval and Renaissance Studies*, 3 (1973), 255–71; S. Wenzel, 'The source of the *Remedia* of the *Parson's Tale*', *Traditio*, 27 (1971), 433–56; S. Wenzel, 'The source of Chaucer's seven deadly sins', *Traditio*, 30 (1974), 351–78.

10. See J. Finlayson, 'The satiric mode of the *Parson's Tale*', *Chaucer Review*, 6 (1971), 94–116; and D. Aers, *Chaucer, Langland and the Creative Imagination* (Routledge & Kegan Paul, 1980), pp. 108–14.

Chapter 4

1. M.A. Gist, *Love and War in the Medieval Romances* (University of Philadelphia Press, 1947), p. 17. See the invaluable introductory study by E. Power, *Medieval Women* (Cambridge U.P., 1975).

2. In J. O'Faolain and L. Martines (eds), *Not in God's Image* (Harper & Row, 1973), pp. 184–5.

3. J.T. Noonan, *Contraception. A History of its Treatment by Catholic Theologians and Canonists* (Harvard U.P., 1966), p. 151.

4. H.A. Kelly, *Love and Marriage in the Age of Chaucer* (Cornell

U.P., 1975), p. 247.

5. Noonan, *Contraception*, pp. 196, 248–54.
6. *Confessionale*, section 'Concerning the lechery of married couples', translated in T.N. Tentler, *Sin and Confession on the Eve of the Reformation* (Princeton, 1977), p. 176.
7. See discussion at the end of Chapter 3 and references in notes 9 and 10 to that chapter.
8. See *The Book of Margery Kempe*, ed. S.B. Meech (Early English Text Society, o.s. 212, 1940). And S. Delany, 'Sexual economics, Chaucer's Wife of Bath and the Book of Margery Kempe', *Minnesota Review*, 5 (1975), 104–15.
9. Alfred David, *The Strumpet Muse. Art and Morals in Chaucer's Poetry* (Indiana U.P., 1976), Chapter 9.
10. Noonan, *Contraception*, pp. 256–7.
11. See Kate Millett, *Sexual Politics* (Abacus, 1972): on Lawrence, Chapter 5.
12. See R. Boase, *The Origin and Meaning of Courtly Love* (Manchester U.P., 1977); Power, *Medieval Women*, Chapters 1–2; P.M. Kean, *Chaucer and the Making of English Poetry* (Routledge & Kegan Paul, 1972), vol. 1, pp. 166–72. Perhaps the most searching introduction to the subject is Toril Moi's essay 'Desire in language: Andreas Capillanus and the controversy of courtly love', in *Medieval Literature*, ed., David Aers (Harvester, 1986).
13. *The Book of the Knight of the Tower*, ed. M.Y. Offord (Early English Text Society, s.s.2, 1971), p. 164.
14. J. Huizinga, *The Waning of the Middle Ages* (Penguin, 1965), p. 138.
15. A. Gaylord, 'The promises in *The Franklin's Tale*', ELH, 31 (1964), 331–65.
16. For a further discussion of this, see D. Aers, *Chaucer, Langland and the Creative Imagination* (Routledge & Kegan Paul, 1980), pp. 118–24.
17. Aers, *Chaucer, Langland*, pp. 128–42.
18. See the analysis in the following essays: Elizabeth Salter, '*Troilus and Criseyde*: a reconsideration', in *Patterns of Love and Courtesy*, ed. J. Lawlor (Arnold, 1966), pp. 86–106; M.E. McAlpine, *The Genre of Troilus and Criseyde* (Cornell U.P., 1978), pp. 177–81, 235–46; Aers, *Chaucer, Langland*, pp. 139–42.

Brief Chronology of Chaucer's Life and Writings

Life

Probably born some time between 1340 and 1344, Chaucer was the son of a London vintner, one of the urban patriciate. Around 1357 he was serving in the household of the Countess of Ulster, wife of King Edward III's third son. In 1359 he fought in France, was captured and ransomed. From 1360 to 1367 nothing is known of his life, but in 1367 he received an annuity of £20 as valet of the chamber from Edward III and between 1367 and 1386 he is linked with the Royal household. His wife, Philippa, was a lady in the chamber of Edward III's queen, Philippa, while her sister, Katherine Swynford, widowed in 1372, became mistress to the immensely powerful John of Gaunt (fourth son of the King), eventually becoming his third wife in 1396. Both Chaucer's wife and Chaucer received annuities from Gaunt (as in 1374). It seems certain that after 1374 Chaucer no longer lived with his wife.

From 1374 to 1386 Chaucer had an accountant's job as controller of customs and subsidies of wool for the port of London and in 1382 he became controller of the petty customs on wines. In summer 1381 the English Rising took place and converged on Chaucer's London. In 1385 Chaucer found himself a deputy as controller of customs and became a JP in Kent. In 1386 he was an MP. Some consider the struggles between Richard II and groups of his magnates in the mid-1380s may account for Chaucer's loss of the post of controller of customs in 1386, but evidence is minimal: it is worth noting that Chaucer's admirer Usk (with others) was executed in these struggles (1388). Certainly Chaucer was made clerk of the King's Works when Richard II gained control over aristocratic opposition and assumed personal rule; in 1390 he gained the sinecure of sub-forester of Petherton Park, and in 1394 Richard II gave him an annuity. This annuity was doubled on the day of Henry IV's coronation in 1399 after the violent deposition of Richard II and in December of that year Chaucer took a 53-year lease on a house in Westminster Close, dying soon after in October 1400.

One incident should perhaps be recorded although the evidence has been claimed to be more ambiguous than it might seem: in May 1380 Chaucer was legally released for the 'raptus' (rape?) of Cecily Champain.

Writings

The following dates are often speculation and in the case of early datings for some of the *Canterbury Tales*, wholly speculative.

1368–69	*Book of the Duchess.*
1370	By then, translation of part of the *Romance of the Rose.*
1372–80	Writing later to be incorporated in the *Canterbury Tales* as *Second Nun's Tale* and some of the *Monk's Tale; Anelida and Arcite.*
1375–82	In this period, probably, *House of Fame* and *Parliament of Fowls.*
1380–86	Writing later to be incorporated in the *Canterbury Tales: Knight's Tale, Parson's Tale, Man of Law's Tale, Physician's Tale,* perhaps *Manciple's Tale.*

1381–85 Translation of Boethius, *Consolation of Philosophy: Troilus and Criseyde* written during this period.

1385–86 *Legend of Good Women.*

1386 onwards—*The Canterbury Tales*, unfinished and fragmentary, very much work in progress when he died in 1400.

1391–92 *Astrolabe.*

1392 *Equatories of the Planets.*

1393–1400 The neo-stoic Boethian short poems and the short poems to Scogan, Bukton and the 'Complaint to his Purse'.

Suggestions for Further Reading

On the Activity of Reading and Criticism

Aers, D., ed., *Medieval Literature* (Harvester, 1986).

Bakhtin, M.M., *The Dialogic Imagination* (University of Texas, 1981).

Eagleton, T., *Literary Theory* (Blackwell, 1983).

Fish, S.E., *Is There a Text in this Class? The authority of interpretative communities* (Harvard U.P., 1980).

Fowler, R.G. and others, *Language and Contol* (Routledge & Kegan Paul, 1979).

Hodge, R. and Kress, G., *Language as Ideology* (Routledge & Kegan Paul, 1979).

Jameson, F., *Marxism and Form* (Princeton, U.P., 1971).

Jauss, H.R., *Towards an Aesthetic of Reception* (University of Minnesota, 1982).

Lentricchia, F., *After the New Criticism* (Methuen, 1983).

Lentricchia, F., *Criticism and Social Change* (University of Chicago, 1984).

Marcuse, H., *The Aesthetic Dimension* (Macmillan, 1979).

Nuttall, A.D., *A New Mimesis* (Methuen, 1983).

Volosinov, V.N. [Bakhtin, M.M.], *Marxism and the Philosophy of Language* (Seminar Press, 1973).

Towards the Social Contexts of Chaucer's writing

Bolton, J.L., *The Medieval English Economy, 1150–1500* (Dent, 1980).

Brenner, R., 'Agrarian class structure and economic development in pre-industrial Europe', *Past and Present*, 70 (1976), 30–75.

Brenner, R. 'The agrarian roots of European capitalism', *Past and Present*, 97 (1982), 16–113.

Dobson, R.B. (ed.), *The Peasant's Revolt* (Macmillian, 1970)

Dronke, P., *Women Writers of the Middle Ages* (Cambridge U.P., 1984).

Hilton, R., *Bond Men Made Free. Medieval peasant movements and the English uprising of 1381* (Temple Smith, 1973).

Hilton, R., 'Feudalism and the origins of capitalism', *History Workshop*, 1 (1976), 9–25.

Hilton, R. *The English Peasantry in the Later Middle Ages* (Oxford U.P., 1975).

Le Goff, J., *Time, Work and Culture in the Middle Ages* (Chicago, U.P., 1980).

Lerner, R.E., *The Age of Adversity* (Cornell U.P., 1968).

McFarlane, A. *The Origins of English Individualism* (Blackwell, 1978).

McFarlane, K.B., *Lancastrian Kings and Lollard Knights*, Part II (Oxford U.P., 1972).

Miskimin, H.A., *The Economy of Early Renaissance Europe* (Prentice-Hall, 1969).

Postan, M., *Essays on Medieval Agriculture and General Problems of the Medieval Economy* (Cambridge U.P., 1973).

Postan, M., *The Medieval Economy and Society* (Weidenfeld, 1972).

Power, E., *Medieval Women* (Cambridge U.P., 1975).

Rorig, F., *The Medieval Town* (California U.P., 1969).

Thrupp, S.L., *The Merchant Class of Medieval London* (Michigan U.P., 1962).

Tuck, A., *Richard II and the English Nobility* (Arnold, 1973).

Towards the Religious and Intellectual Contexts

Bettenson, H., *Documents of the Christian Church* (Oxford U.P., 1977).

Gilchrist, J., *The Church and Economic Activity in the Middle Ages* (Macmillan, 1969).

Lagarde, G. de, *La naissance de l'esprit laïque*, vol. 5 (Nauwelaerts, 1963).

Lambert, M.D., *Medieval Heresy* (Arnold, 1977).

Leff, G., *Heresy in the Later Middle Ages*, 2 vols (Manchester U.P., 1967).

Leff, G., *The Dissolution of the Medieval Outlook* (Harper & Row, 1976).

Manning, B.L., *The People's Faith in the Time of Wyclif* (Cambridge, U.P., 1917).

McGrade, A.S., *The Political Thought of William of Ockham* (Cambridge U.P., 1974).

Noonan, J.T., *Contraception. A history of its treatment by Catholic theologians and canonists* (Harvard U.P., 1963).

Oberman, H.A., *The Harvest of Medieval Theology* (Harvard U.P., 1963).

Pantin, W.A., *The English Church in the Fourteenth Century* (Cambridge U.P., 1955).

Southern, R.W., *Western Society and the Church in the Middle Ages* (Penguin, 1970).

Toussaert, J. *Le Sentiment Religieux en Flandre à la fin du Moyen Age* (Plon, Paris, 1963).

Trinkaus, C., and Oberman, H.A. (eds), *The Pursuit of Holiness* (Brill, 1974).

Wakefield, W.L. and Evans, A.P., *Heresies of the High Middle*

Ages, (Columbia U.P., 1969).

Wilks, M.J., *The Problem of Sovereignty in the Later Middle Ages* (Cambridge, U.P., 1964).

Suggestions Towards Reading some Contemporary Texts

Andrew, M.R. and Waldron, R., (eds), *The Poems of the Pearl Manuscript* (Arnold, 1978).

Boccaccio, G., *Il Filostrato*: translated in *The Story of Troilus* (Dutton, 1964).

Bryan, W.F. and Dempster, G., *Sources and Analogues of Chaucer's Canterbury Tales* (Routledge & Kegan Paul, 1958).

Christine de Pisan, *The Book of the City of Ladies*, transl. E.J. Richards (Picador, 1983).

Clanvowe, John, *The Works*, ed. V.J. Scattergood (Brewer Press, 1976).

Gower, John, *Vox Clamantis*, trans. E.W. Stockton, in *The Major Latin Works of Gower* (Washington U.P., 1962).

Hudson, A. (ed.), *English Wyclyfite Writings* (Cambridge U.P., 1978).

Julian of Norwich, *A Book of Showings*, ed. E. Colledge and J. Walsh, 2 vols (Pontifical Institute of Medieval Studies, Toronto, 1978).

Kempe, Margery, *The Book of Margery Kempe*, ed. S.B. Meech and H.E. Allen (Early English Text Society, o-s. 212, 1940; reprinted 1961).

Langland, William, *Piers Plowman. The B. Version*, ed. G. Kane and E.T. Donaldson (Athlone Press, 1975).

Langland, William, *Piers Plowman: an edition of the C-text*, ed. Derek Pearsall (Arnold, 1978).

O'Faolain, J. and Martines, L. (eds), *Not In God's Image: Women in History*, sections 5–8 (Fontana, 1974).

Robbins, R.H. (ed.), *Historical Poems of the Fourteenth and*

Fifteenth Century (Oxford U.P., 1959).
York Plays, ed. R. Beadle (Arnold, 1981).

On Chaucer

Aers, D., *Chaucer, Langland and the Creative Imagination* (Routledge & Kegan Paul, 1980).

David, A., *The Strumpet Muze. Art and Morals in Chaucer's Poetry* (Indiana U.P., 1976).

Delany, S., *Chaucer's House of Fame* (Chicago U.P., 1972).

Delany, S., *Writing Woman* (Schocken, 1983).

Elbow, P., *Opposition in Chaucer* (Wesleyan U.P., 1975).

Ferster, J., *Chaucer on Interpretation* (Cambridge U.P., 1985).

Howard, D.R., *The Idea of the Canterbury Tales* (California U.P., 1976)

Knight, S., 'Chaucer and the sociology of literature', *Studies in the Age of Chaucer*, 2 (1980), 15–51.

Knight, S., 'Ideology in *The Franklin's Tale*', *Parergon*, 28 (1980), 3–35.

Knight, S., *Chaucer* (Blackwell, 1986).

Kolve, V.A., *Chaucer and the Imagery of Narrative* (Arnold, 1984)

Mann, J., *Chaucer and Medieval Estates Satire* (Cambridge U.P., 1973).

Muscatine, C., *Chaucer and the French Tradition* (California U.P., 1964).

Salter, E., *Chaucer: The Knight's Tale and The Clerk's Tale* (Arnold, 1962).

Salter, E., '*Troilus and Criseyde*: a reconsideration', in *Patterns of Love and Courtesy*, ed. J. Lawlor (Arnold, 1966).

Salter, E., *Fourteenth-Century English Poetry* (Oxford U.P., 1983).

Spearing, A.C., *Chaucer: Troilus and Criseyde* (Arnold, 1976).

Strohm, P., 'Chaucer's audience', *Literature and History*, 5 (1977) 26–41.

Two Extremely Helpful Introductions to the Period's Writing

Coleman, J., *Medieval Writers and Readers* (Hutchinson, 1981).

Pearsall, D.A., *Old and Middle English Poetry* (Routledge & Kegan Paul, 1977).

Index